Thomas of the Creator

Donald G. Boland

En Route Books and Media, LLC

Saint Louis, MO USA

⊕ENROUTE
Make the time

En Route Books and Media, LLC

5705 Rhodes Avenue

St. Louis, MO 63109

Contact us at **contact@enroutebooksandmedia.com**

Cover Credit: An original oil painting (970mm x 1220mm on wood with a wood frame) of St. Thomas Aquinas by Australian artist Barbara Hearn (1953) located at Campion College in Toongabbie, New South Wales, Australia. The painting was executed at the request of the Very Rev Dr Austin Woodbury, SM, the regent at the time of Aquinas Academy in The Rocks, New South Wales, Australia. The author is grateful to Dr Paul Morrissey, president of Campion College, for granting permission to use this image as the cover of this book.

Special thanks to Frank Calneggia for his editing of this book.

ISBN-13: 979-8-88870-093-8

Library of Congress Control Number: 2023946406

Dedication

To Giacomo della Chiesa
Pope Benedict XV, "The Pope of Peace"

Sometimes referred to as the unknown pope but in his short pontificate of 7 years, despite most of it being during the period of The Great War he worked with a remarkable degree of intense activity and achieved more than most, not just in the cause of peace but also in the improvement of many areas of the life of the Church.

He was known as the missionary pope and re-established many institutions that had been broken by political ruptures in Europe. His record of encyclicals is extraordinary producing within a short period twelve most commemorating important historical figures, such as St. Boniface, the apostle of Germany, St. Ephrem, who he made a doctor of the Church, much to the joy of the Eastern faithful. He wrote an encyclical on the centenary anniversaries of St. Jerome and St. Dominic and not to confine his admiration for ecclesiastical figures celebrated the life and legacy of Dante Alighieri in a wonderful encyclical. He canonized St. Joan of Arc, patron of France.

We have quoted much from his first encyclical (Nov. 1914) connecting the causes of the dreadful events of the first part of the twentieth century to the godlessness that had descended on modern civilization as a result of the rejection of divine authority. It was his depth of insight into current and historical events and also his foresight of even worse to come that makes his pontificate most relevant to our subject matter.

Quotations

There is also, however, a theological concealment of the concept of creation which, causally, is probably connected with the two previous concealments. Here nature is undermined for the sake of grace; it is robbed of its belongings and gives way, so to speak, before grace. Here we should recall the crucial text of 1 Corinthians 15: 46: 'It is not the spiritual which is first but the physical and then the spiritual' (RSV). There is a series of stages that must not be absorbed into a monism of grace. I believe that we must develop a Christian pedagogy that accepts creation and gives concrete expression to these two poles of the one faith. We must never try to take the second step before the first: first the physical, then the spiritual. If we skip this sequence, creation is denied, and grace is deprived of its foundation". (Cardinal Ratzinger, *In the Beginning*, p. 94)

"Most modern freedom is at root fear. It is not so much that we are too bold to endure rules; it is rather that we are too timid to endure responsibilities." G.K. Chesterton – "Authority the Unavoidable," *What's Wrong With the World*.

As for quotes relevant to the foolishness of those who say in their heart of hearts 'there is no God', one could fill a library with quotes from the works of G K Chesterton and indeed find as many as one could wish for in any one of his individual collections of articles. We need only to use here a selection from the very last such book, "The Well and the Shallows". There is one article entitled "The Backward Bolshie" (p. 96) which could be used to show how backward is modern atheism in Capitalism and Communism.

For his point that today's Communist, as was Marx himself, is trying to adjust the thinking of the Victorians of the nineteenth century, by which name is intended the believers in Capitalism, another name for the religion of the rich. Modern Economic Science is in my view a disguised form of the old religion of Mammon, the love of money, as noted by Pope Benedict XV, in modern dress.

The Chinese Communist Party is the latest effort to adopt a philosophy/religion more ancient than Confucius. They can look down on the collectivity of their corporate/bureaucratic ancestors in the West, which is hardly more than a corrupting body on its last legs. That is not to deny there is much good in modern society in West and East. But this is from the created goodness that is in human nature (as redeemed) that is able to survive, as Adam Smith put it, not only the ravages of the disease it is subjected to but even the absurd prescriptions of its [secularist] doctors.

With regard to the question of the opposed views of history and philosophy with which we are primarily concerned here, we will select just one quote from the book in which there is a section from which the title of the book has been taken, *The Well and the Shallows.* (p. 58) "That is really the crux of the controversy between the two views of history and philosophy. If it were true that by leaving the temple we walked out into a world of truths, the question would be answered; but it is not true. By leaving the temple, we walk out into a world of idols; and the idols of the marketplace are more perishable and passing than the gods of the temple we have left. If we wished to test rationally the case of rationalism, we should follow the career of the sceptic and ask how far he remained sceptical about the idols or ideals of the world into which he went. There are very few sceptics in history who cannot be proved to have been instantly swallowed by some swollen convention or some hungry humbug of the hour, so that all their utterances about contemporary things now look to us almost pathetically contemporary. The little group of Atheists, who still run their paper in Fleet Street and frequently honour me with hearty but somewhat hasty denunciation, began their agitation in the old Victorian days, and selected for themselves a terribly appropriate title. They did not call themselves Atheists, they called themselves Secularists. Never was a more bitter and blighting confession made in the form of a boast. For the word 'secular' does not mean anything so sensible as 'worldly'. It does not even mean anything so spirited as 'irreligious'. To be secular simply means to be of the age; that is, of the age which is passing; of the age which, in their case, is already passed. There is one tolerably correct translation of the Latin word which they have chosen as their motto. There is one adequate equivalent of the word 'secular'; and it is the word 'dated'."

Table of Contents

Preface

The subject matter of this book could be given various titles. It is really part of Metaphysics, which, though one and undivided, can be studied from three aspects. It is first of all the study of being (*ens*) as being, or of being in common, taken as the first object of the human intellect. Indeed, the human intellect may be referred to simply as the faculty of being, just as the human eye might be called the faculty of the primary object of seeing, which is colour. A better way of putting it would be that the object of sight is being as coloured. For, as St. Thomas says, all knowledge is of being. It is just that other than Metaphysics the object is being according to some particular aspect. It is only Metaphysics that studies being in all its universality. Yet even here as we will see when we deal with Logic that universality is not to be taken univocally.

Thus, when we take being as being, there are these three aspects mentioned that go by the special names of Ontology, Natural Theology and Epistemology. For, being as the object of the human intellect can be considered in itself and in its relation to its cause, which is God, and to its effect, which is truth in the human intellect.

There is no difficulty in seeing that here we are concerned with Natural Theology. The reason for dealing with it after Ontology and before Epistemology has already been explained. Another name for it is the philosophy of God. We need to be careful with the word "theology" as there is total confusion over the use of the word not only by modern philosophers and scientists, who know no metaphysics, but also by modern Catholic theologians whose hold on

vii

philosophy has never been weaker (cf. *Fides et ratio, n. 61)*. We have painful experience of this deficiency in moral philosophy in the most critical social area in the modern world with regard to politico-economic affairs. But we will see this serious deficiency pointed up by former Pope Benedict XVI himself in regard to the very study of God. We will come shortly to his important work in this regard ("In the Beginning").

Metaphysics is philosophy, and so natural theology is a philosophical study. Because of their weakness in Metaphysics many Catholic theologians (especially the more "innovative") can hardly distinguish between the metaphysical and the supernatural, so that natural theology has disappeared from their vocabulary. The same problem is had with the word "spiritual". There is much difficulty therefore with getting Catholic "intellectuals" and academics to keep to the level of philosophy and away from the error of fideism or supernaturalism.

The other thing to keep to in the study of philosophy is the distinction between the theoretical and the practical, with especial attention to the distinction between Metaphysics and Ethics. Where the discussion of God is concerned, as we shall see, there is much mixing up of the two, Even in the philosophical study of God the practical tends to dominate. Yet, Natural Theology as part of Metaphysics is a theoretical study of God, his existence and nature. In this context the use of the words "belief" and "faith" need to be carefully analysed, as they are full of equivocations even without those introduced within the discussion of matters religious in modern secularist culture.

We have given particular attention to the mess made of the study of religion in modern Sociology derived from Durkheim, developed by such as Weber, and given a peculiar twist by Charles Taylor. (cf. our separate review of his book "A Secular Age").

But let us deal first with the neglect of the study of God as creator in Catholic studies of recent times that former Pope Benedict XVI referred to most pointedly in his book "In the Beginning". It seems no coincidence that it occurs with the neglect of philosophy generally by theologians since Vatican II that Pope Saint John Paul II referred to in *Fides et ratio* (*n. 61*). This too may be readily connected with the lamentable neglect of the study of Aquinas, despite the continued insistence of the Magisterium of paying special attention to Aquinas not only in theology but also in philosophy.

The disobedience of the theological faculties even in those universities purporting to be Catholic is reprehensible, but for some strange reason not reprehended. It is as if the Catholic academic world has wholly succumbed to the secularist philosophy that dominates the educational world of the West and has issued its own declaration of independence from episcopal and even papal authority. The reason for this may be gathered from the books we have published already. But it will become even more evident with this and our following books.

It will be seen when we come to examine more closely the work of Pope Benedict why we have decided to adopt as the title for our book the simple one of "Thomas of the Creator". This enables us to highlight the great common doctor of the Church on the cover page. For, there is no greater defender of God, not just as the author of nature as physical but also as metaphysical.

With regard to the title let us simply give the quote of Pope Benedict: "G. K. Chesterton was often blessed with the gift of a striking turn of phrase. He certainly hit upon a decisive aspect of the work of St. Thomas Aquinas when he observed that, if the great doctor were to be given a name in the style of the Carmelite Order ('... of the Child Jesus,' 'of the Mother of God,' etc.), he would have to be called *Thomas a Creatore* - 'Thomas of the Creator.' Creator and creation are the core of his theological thought. It says something for the thesis that it was only with the full intellectual penetration of faith in creation that the Christian penetration of the inheritance of antiquity reached its goal. That is why the theme of creation suggests itself for a celebration of St. Thomas." (pp. 79-80)

The cardinal at the time who went on to become pope immediately noted the connection between the neglect of the study of Aquinas and that of creation by contemporary theologians, going back decades; this he says in the 1980's which means at least since the Council. "However, just as St. Thomas and his theology have become distant from us, so, until recently, the theme of creation has been far from central to contemporary theological thinking. In fact, the theme of creation has played only a small role in the theological discussion of recent years, indeed decades." (p. 80)

To appreciate the pungency of the criticism it is worth quoting in full the short Author's note.

"For the practical abandonment of the doctrine of creation in influential modern theology I would like to mention here just two significant examples. In J. Feiner and L. Fischer, eds., *Neues Glaubensbuch. Degemeinsame christliche Glaube* (Basil-Zurich, 1973), the theme of creation is hidden away in a chapter devoted to 'History and Cosmos,' which in turn belongs to the fourth part of the book, entitled 'Faith and World.' The three previous parts deal with 'The Question of God,' 'God in Jesus Christ,' and 'The New Human Being.' One dare not hope for anything more positive from this arrangement, but the text itself, by A. Dumas and O. H. Pesch, goes beyond one's worst fears. The reader discovers here phrases such as 'Concepts like selection and mutation are intellectually much more honest than that of creation' (p. 433); '*Creation* as a cosmic plan is an idea that has seen its day' (ibid.); 'The concept of creation is withal an unreal concept' (p. 435); 'Creation means a call addressed to the human being. Whatever else may be said about it, even in the Bible, is not the message of creation itself but rather its partly mythological and apocalyptic formulation' (pp. 435-36). Would it be too harsh to say that the continued use of the term 'creation" against the background of these presuppositions represents a semantic betrayal?

The same reductionist position, less crassly formulated, appears in *La foi des catholiques. Catechise fondamentale* (Paris, 1984). This 736-page work dedicates five full pages to the theme of creation. These are found in the third part, under the heading 'Humanity according to the Gospel.' (The first two parts are entitled 'A Living Faith' and 'The Christian Revelation.') Creation is defined as follows: 'Thus, in speaking of God as Creator, it is affirmed that the first and final meaning of life is to be found in God himself, most intimately present to our being' (p. 356). Here, too, the term 'creation' has completely lost its original meaning. Moreover, in type different from that which appears in the rest of the text and which is otherwise used for lengthy citations or supplementary texts, the 'current objections to creation' are presented in four points, to which the average reader (myself included) can find no response in the text. He would then have to reinterpret creation in an existential sense. With such an 'existential' reduction of the creation theme, however, there occurs a huge (if not a total) loss of the reality of the faith, whose God no longer has anything to do with matter." (pp. x-xii)

There could be no more damning indictment of Catholic theologians of his day. Here again, however, if anything, the situation has gotten worse since. An index of the powerful influence of modern "scientific" thinking on the minds of contemporary theologians, as with all modern "educated" people, Catholic or otherwise, can be seen in the footnotes Pope Benedict cites.

The indoctrination in science as limited to mathematics and physics and the material order of reality is all but complete. Paradoxically, whereas true science and wisdom is focused on forms that bespeak limits, the modern notion of science is more focused on formlessness and infinity. Such a view of the world induces vertigo, as of one floating in a void. It is as if a spell has been cast over the modern mind, and the Catholic, though inoculated against it, is not fully free of its diabolical power. We have alluded to this already, but will come to it more tellingly in the books that follow.

Here we focus on one effect of this staring into blank space – like a fool. This raises a distinction we have already alluded to, namely between theoretical and practical knowledge, or more pertinently between natural wisdom (Metaphysics) and practical wisdom (Ethics). It is a nice distinction where belief in God is concerned. Nonetheless, it is one we ought not gloss over.

We are concerned here with what belongs to Metaphysics and theoretical truth. What is God, does he exist? Psalm 14 says: "The fool says in his heart there is no God". That looks as if it is saying that the atheist is a fool. But, just as wisdom is of two kinds, theoretical and practical, so fool has a different connotation when taken in a metaphysical and in a moral sense. The phrase "in his heart" points to the activity of choice, for "heart" refers to the whole being or soul of man, which is derived finally by the state of one's will. The seeing of God as one's ultimate good follows almost immediately from the understanding of God as the cause of one's being.

But there can be a disconnection, so that, for instance, one is excused from moral fault by invincible ignorance. Though at the deepest level of the natural moral law it is difficult to believe that one can be totally excused (short of insanity) the blameworthiness can be reduced significantly by extrinsic factors, such as poor education and upbringing. Throughout human history pure atheism was a rarity.

The modern age is particularly noteworthy by the spread of atheism. Is it a coincidence that this has accompanied the dominance of modern science? Hardly. But what is the reason? To us it is to do with the change in the concept of knowledge. The scientist (and professed philosopher), insofar as he is committed to the modern notion of science, has explicitly excluded natural wisdom as science. To this he connects the rejection of Aristotelian science not just in Metaphysics but also wholesale including Natural Science (along with which goes Mathematics and even Aristotle's notion of physico-mathematics).

There is simply no place in the notion of modern science for holding any truth about God, including whether he exists. Outer space has been explored by the most sophisticated means of detection and there is no "evidence" of any kind of God. When Aquinas says that God is not a body the scientist scratches his head. Do you mean to say there is no observable evidence for such a being? Let us then get down to the real business of knowing what is scientifically verifiable and technically creatable.

The atheist scientist can become quite indignant if it is suggested that he is morally at fault for not believing in God. He is just as moral as the next person. Indeed, he will not see himself as self-centered but dedicated to the improvement of the lot his fellow man. And he has a point – theoretically. You must prove "scientifically" to me that God exists if you demand I believe in him. That is what all regard as intellectual honesty.

How well founded morally that attitude is, is another matter. Can he really plead invincible ignorance of knowing that the invisible God exists and is Lord of all from the things that are visible? St. Paul says he has no excuse. The obligation of religion is a basic one of natural justice that even without knowledge of the Law (as revealed) is the absolutely first of moral obligations. It may be necessary to have a rational proof of the existence of this God but it is almost self-evident. Most children have no difficulty with it until they are exposed to modern education.

Nonetheless, there is a real difficulty for us living in the modern era. St. Paul was speaking before the second round, as it were, of paganism, in which Chesterton observes the modern sins such as of avarice and lust are of a magnitude of evil that dwarfs those of the pre-Christian era ("infinitely worse "is how he puts it in his article on Property and Sex in "The Well and the Shallows"). The modern proclivity to sin seems to be fortified by a level of diabolic deception previously not had. We might then at least allow that the modern mind's concept of God is so fundamentally distorted that there may be some excuse that diminishes moral fault even of the deepest depravity, if it cannot totally exculpate.

This has to be taken into account when we come to consider the five ways of St. Thomas. To his mind they are so evident that he sets out in summary fashion the whole five in one question of the *Summa Theologiae* (of 550 + questions).Yet modern day professed followers of St. Thomas will be preoccupied in finding objections and difficulties to one or other of the proofs. Generally such difficulties can be connected with concepts of time motion and causality much affected by their education in modern science. The concept of motion, for instance, is given a mathematical motionlessness that distorts one's understanding of the first way. This was made much use of by Sir Anthony Kenny, a leading Oxford University authority on Aquinas.

We will pay some attention to these objections but we are mainly concerned with setting out the proofs and justifying them in their own terms, which, even though they start from sensible experience, and seem to some having to be dealt with in physical scientific terms, ultimately need to be understood metaphysically. Natural Theology is part of Metaphysics. We are concerned with the cause of being as being, not with a prime mover, a first cause, a necessary being, a most perfect form of being or a last end in physical terms.

Thomas of the Creator

Some have foolishly (in the theoretical sense) tried to maintain that we cannot do Metaphysics until we have proved from Physics that the spiritual order of reality exists. Here they talk vaguely not appreciating that the only apodictic proof of a purely spiritual being is of God. So we cannot do Metaphysics (Ontology) until we have done Natural Theology! Talk about putting the cart before the horse. It is somewhat like the modern assertion that being is part of our knowledge and we have to find a way out to the real world (by that wonderful mental construct called the bridge of knowledge). But in our treatment this interesting (pseudo) problem comes next in our book on Epistemology.

Before addressing directly the question of the existence of God as dealt with by St. Thomas, we will expand a little more on Pope Benedict's critique of modern theologian's treatment, or lack thereof, of the question of creation.

The pope goes to some length in an appendix of about 20 pages in an endeavor to explain how the discussion of God as creator has dropped out of contemporary theology. He acknowledges that such a historical overview as he makes is necessarily fragmentary but focuses on three key figures in modern times, Giordano Bruno, Galileo Galilei and Martin Luther, thus drawing together three lines of influence, philosophical, scientific and theological. Others have focused on other major figures, such as Maritain did on Descartes, Rousseau and Luther. There are all sorts of lines one could take and there is something to be gotten from all. The pope brings in Hegel and Marx.

It is to be expected that the development of things to the present stage of history is a matter of great complexity, just as the pathological progress of a diseased constitution is necessarily so. There is a simple explanation to which we have already adverted and all these complex factors point back to it, namely, the public and personal rejection made throughout Europe including the British Isles at the beginning of the modern age of the divine authority of the Church instituted by Christ as God to complete the salvation of mankind.

Nothing can go smoothly in this world but everything had to go radically awry following this and this took a multitude of forms too many to trace. It meant the turning of human thought and love upon itself and was thus a modern replay by a great proportion of mankind of the original retort of Adam and Eve deceived by Lucifer to God in his Church, *non serviam*. This rebellion by modern man against God's Church inevitably brought its evil consequences not just supernaturally but also naturally, as the natural nemesis that follows injustice, which came to a dramatic head at the beginning of the twentieth century. The mark of Satan, the father of lies and a murderer from the beginning, is all over the subsequent events into our own time.

We have dedicated this book to Pope Benedict XV whose pontificate began just as the First World War broke out and ended only shortly after it was concluded. He gives a masterly analysis of the causes of the "war to end all wars" which he feared signaled the end of modern civilization. This he did in his first encyclical (1 Nov. 1914). First, he refers to the horrors of the war in the most graphic terms: "3. But as soon as we were able from the height of Apostolic dignity to survey at a glance the course of human affairs, our eyes were met by the sad conditions of human society, and we could not but be filled with bitter sorrow. For what could prevent the soul of the common Father of all being most deeply distressed by the spectacle presented by Europe, nay, by the whole world, perhaps the saddest and most mournful spectacle of which there is any record. Certainly those days would seem to have come upon us of which Christ Our Lord foretold: 'You shall hear of wars and rumours of wars - for nation shall rise against nation, and kingdom against kingdom' (*Matt.* xxiv, 6, 7). On every side the dread phantom of war holds sway: there is scarce room for another thought in the minds of men. **The combatants are the greatest and wealthiest nations of the earth; what wonder, then, if, well provided with the most awful weapons modern military science has devised, they strive to destroy one another with refinements of horror.** There is no limit to the measure of ruin and of slaughter; day by day the earth is drenched with newly-shed blood, and is covered with the bodies of the wounded and of the slain. Who would imagine as we see them thus filled with hatred of one another, that they are all of one common stock, all of the same nature, all members of the same human society? Who would recognize brothers, whose Father is in Heaven? Yet, while with numberless troops the furious battle is engaged, the sad cohorts of war, sorrow and distress swoop down upon every city and every home; day by day the mighty number of widows and orphans increases, and with the interruption of communications, trade is at a standstill; agriculture is abandoned; the arts are reduced to inactivity; the wealthy are in difficulties; the poor are reduced to abject misery; all are in distress." (bold added)

That is the general picture. It is the working part of the population within these greatest and wealthiest nations that were sent to be slaughtered in their millions – for what purpose we would need to more closely examine. But the pope puts his mind to the more spiritual and deeper, if historically seemingly remote, aspects of the cause of the war.

"5. But it is not the present sanguinary strife alone that distresses the nations and fills Us with anxiety and care. There is another evil raging in the very inmost heart of human society, a source of dread to all who really think, inasmuch as it has already brought, and will bring, many misfortunes upon nations, and may rightly be considered to be the root cause of the present awful war. **For ever since the precepts and practices of Christian wisdom ceased to be observed in the ruling of states, it followed that, as they contained the peace and stability of institutions, the very foundations of states necessarily began to be shaken.** Such, moreover, has been the change in the ideas and the morals of men, that unless God comes soon to our help, the end of civilization would seem to be at hand. Thus we see [1] the absence from the relation of men of mutual love with their fellow men; [2] the authority of rulers is held in contempt; [3] injustice reigns in relations between the classes of society; [4] the striving for transient and perishable things is so keen, that men have lost sight of the other and more worthy goods they have to obtain. It is under these four headings that may be grouped, We consider, the causes of the serious unrest pervading the whole of human society. All then must combine to get rid of them by again bringing Christian principles into honour, if We have any real desire for the peace and harmony of human society." (bold and numbers added)

The pope then makes an interesting observation that we could apply to our own day: the sad gap between talk of dialogue and fraternity and the evident absence of realization in action. "7. Far different from this is the behaviour of men today. Never perhaps was there more talking about the brotherhood of men than there is today; in fact, men do not hesitate to proclaim that striving after brotherhood is one of the greatest gifts of modern civilization, ignoring the teaching of the Gospel, and setting aside the work of Christ and of His Church. But in reality never was there less brotherly activity amongst men than at the present moment. Race hatred has reached its climax; peoples are more divided by jealousies than by frontiers; within one and the same nation, within the same city there rages the burning envy of class against class; and amongst individuals it is self-love which is the supreme law over-ruling everything."

The second cause referred to is that which applies most directly to the rejection of divine authority but which has naturally spilled over into contempt for human authority. This has an obvious connection with the ideology of Liberalism that came to dominate political philosophy from the beginning of the modern era, but has its source in the modern "Declaration of Independence" from all authority over individuals' "freedom". At the end he makes reference to the rise of the ideology of Socialism/Communism, saying that he does not intend to repeat in this document the arguments of his predecessors. The clash of the two opposed ideologies of Capitalism and Communism will of course dominate the rest of the twentieth century.

"9. The second cause of the general unrest we declare to be the absence of respect for the authority of those who exercise ruling powers. Ever since the source of human powers has been sought apart from God the Creator and Ruler of the Universe, in the free will of men, the bonds of duty, which should exist between superior and inferior, have been so weakened as almost to have ceased to exist. The unrestrained striving after independence, together with over-weening pride, has little by little found its way everywhere; it has not even spared the home, although the natural origin of the ruling power in the family is as clear as the noonday sun; nay, more deplorable still, it has not stopped at the steps of the sanctuary. Hence come contempt for laws, insubordination of the masses, wanton criticism of orders issued, hence innumerable ways of undermining authority; hence, too, the terrible crimes of men who, claiming to be bound by no laws, do not hesitate to attack the property or the lives of their fellow men."

We do not wish to go into the relative importance of these causes, though it is plain enough. Our interest so far has been on causes and effects at the politico-economic level. The pope however does point to the depth of this social cause is a paragraph closely following: "14. But there is still, Venerable Brethren, a deeper root of the evils we have hitherto been deploring, and unless the efforts of good men concentrate on its extirpation, that tranquil stability and peacefulness of human relations we so much desire, can never be attained. The apostle himself tells us what it is: 'The desire of money is the root of all evils' (I. *Tim* vi. 10). If any one considers the evils under which human society is at present labouring, they will all be seen to spring from this root."

Our books have been concerned to give some concrete application to this factor in modern politico-economic history. We have noted however how the attention of Catholic moral theologians has been deflected from its proper consideration, a neglect that has come to be mirrored in contemporary theologians neglect even in the proper consideration of the question of creation, as noted by Pope Benedict XVI.

Pope Benedict XV provides some insight into a profound reason for such neglect within modern public education, namely, its secularist basis to which Catholics in "Western civilization", including those who will become clerics and theologians, are almost unconsciously subjected as well. "15. Once the plastic minds of children have been moulded by godless schools, and the ideas of the inexperienced masses have been formed by a bad daily or periodical press, and when by means of all the other influences which direct public opinion, there has been instilled into the minds of men that most pernicious error that man must not hope for a state of eternal happiness; but that it is here, here below, that he is to be happy in the enjoyment of wealth and honour and pleasure: what wonder that those men whose very nature was made for happiness should with all the energy which impels them to seek that very good, break down whatever delays or impedes their obtaining it. And as these goods are not equally divided amongst men, and as it is the duty of authority in the State to prevent the freedom enjoyed by the individual from going beyond its due limits and invading what belongs to another, it comes to pass that public authority is hated, and the envy of the unfortunate is inflamed against the more fortunate. Thus the struggle of one class of citizen against another bursts forth, the one trying by every means to obtain and to take what they want to have, the other endeavouring to hold and to increase what they possess."

What is more godless than the education in science today that explains all in terms of materialist evolution? And what hope is more instilled in the hapless children than on leaving school that of "getting a job", i. e. "to make money" so that one can afford the pleasures that pass and pay for the medicines (drugs) that dull the pains that inevitably ensue. No wonder the youth are soon depressed.

However, the pope does not dwell on this bleak picture of modern life and points to the true way not only to personal peace but also to national and international peace. What we seek is there for the asking. It is simply a matter of thinking again (repenting) and turning our minds heavenwards where our true home awaits us. "18. Hence it is necessary, Venerable Brethren, to revive it once more in the minds of all, for in no other way can individuals and nations attain to peace. Let us, then, bid those who are undergoing distress of whatever kind, not to cast their eyes down to the earth in which we are as pilgrims, but to raise them to Heaven to which we are going: 'For we have not here a lasting city, but we seek one that is to come' (*Heb.* xiii. 14). In the midst of the adversities whereby God tests their perseverance in His service, let them often think of the reward that is prepared for them if victorious in the trial: 'For that which is at present momentary and light of our tribulation worketh for us above measure exceedingly an eternal weight of glory' (II *Cor.* iv. 17). We must strive by every possible means to revive amongst men faith in the supernatural truths, and at the same time the esteem, the desire and the hope of eternal goods."

This is the message the subsequent popes have continued to repeat, no matter how desperate the picture of mass murder, licentious lust and voracious avarice has become. In the midst of all this misery there lies, unsung of course, the work of the Church in her saintly men and women from scores of selfless laity to shining lights of Catholic life and truth in tireless religious sisters and brothers, and clergy from priests to popes.

But we cannot, however, ignore the forces of evil that abound and the fact that our fight is against "principalities and powers". Here we focus on a particular obstacle (*diabolos*) thrown in our path, which as pointed out by Pope Benedict XVI has caused contemporary Catholic theologians generally to stumble in dealing with our understanding of creation and the importance of seeing God as Creator (as the author of nature) even in treating of Christ as God and Saviour. This is all brought out in the appendix to the book "In the Beginning" to which we refer our readers. Here we will draw particular note only to some striking parts of it.

The pope points to a change of focus from God to man at the time of the "Reformation" and later the shift from creation to evolution as the context in which human nature needed to be considered. And then the focus comes to be on human nature within the domain of nature generally, i.e. as an object of natural science. Then there was the change of interest in human nature as a theoretical object to a matter of practical concern. Thus he says: "Human beings' concentration on doing, on fashioning a new and better world for themselves, has made the resistance to creation stand out with increasing clarity ... Human beings want to understand the discovered world only as material for their own creativity". This we can relate to the aim of science as stated by both Francis Bacon and

Rene Descartes as not knowledge for its own sake but for the sake of production.

Then the pope points to the ironical about-turn in later times of which we are now all too familiar: "the Christian doctrine of creation is now regarded as the pillage of the world". The religious orientation of human nature is the problem, a threat to nature. The pope takes up the matter under a new heading; notice the theological implications: "The Suppression of Faith in Creation in Modern Thought". The theologians' neglect can be directly attributed to "the spirit of modernity". The theologians have been caught short by the influence upon them of this "spirit". This is not fundamentally a theological problem but a metaphysical one (as Pope Saint Pius X clearly saw). So Pope Benedict XVI goes on to examine its historical development, which is where he brings in Bruno, Galileo and Luther.

We are more interested in Galileo from the philosophical level of consideration, for the modern spirit is concreted in the change in the concept of science, its truncation so that it treats the mathematical and empirical/material as the only way to access objective reality. We will not go into here the immediate shift into subjectivism originating in Galileo but taken up by Locke so that not even sensible qualities are real, only quantitatively measurable ones are. But the pope has latched on to the shift in the notion of objectivity to admit only the objects of the new physico-mathematical order of sciences. Instead of Galileo we have preferred to see this shift solidified in Isaac Newton. It is from him that subsequent modern philosophy takes its lead in the "phenomenal" objectivism of Kant and the idealistic subjectivism of Hegel, to which Marx gave the final twist of "praxis".

The pope makes these points: "In Galileo we see the return to Greece, not in its aesthetic and emancipatory form (alluding to Bruno) but in a reversion to the mathematical side of Platonic thought. (We might note the influence of Pythagoras). "'God does geometry' is the way he [Galileo] expresses his concepts of God and nature as well as his scientific ideal. God wrote the book of nature with mathematical letters ... the concept of nature in the sense of the object of science, takes the place of the concept of creation." The pope perceptively notes how this affects the very notion of a first cause. This carries over for a time in the rationalist mathematico-metaphysics of Leibniz and Wolff until "transcended" by Kant.

However, the more immediate theological cause of the neglect of any focus on creation in modern Catholic thought can be traced, as the pope does, to the influence of Luther (not unrelated to Luther's antipathy to reason). Just as Bruno's and Galileo's thinking was a return to the Greek notion of the cosmos, Luther's was a reaction against it. The idea of creation suffered on all three counts. We will not go into the pope's analysis (the reader can do that for himself). But under the sub-heading of "The Concept of Creation in Present-Day Thought: Three Forms of Concealment" this is how he sums up: "1. The concept is concealed by the scientific concept of nature." 2. relates to a resentment against man's domination of nature – civilization has in fact come to be seen as anti-natural, as in Rousseau. Nature as known pure and simple is put on a pedestal, not to be made dependent upon a God as Creator.

However, things get into quite a tangle at this "natural" level. What we are more interested in is what the pope has to say in 3. "There is also, however, a theological concealment of the concept of creation which, causally, is probably connected with the two previous concealments. Here nature is undermined for the sake of grace; it is robbed of its belongings and gives way, so to speak, before grace. Here we should recall the crucial text of 1 Corinthians 15: 46: 'It is not the spiritual which is first but the physical and then the spiritual' (RSV). There is a series of stages that must not be absorbed into a monism of grace. I believe that we must develop a Christian pedagogy that accepts creation and gives concrete expression to these two poles of the one faith. We must never try to take the second step before the first: first the physical, then the spiritual. If we skip this sequence, creation is denied, and grace is deprived of its foundation". (p. 94)

The pope goes on: "This undermining of creation can never become a vehicle of grace, but only of an *odium generis humani*, a Gnostic disenchantment with creation, which ultimately does not and cannot desire grace any longer" ... "However, in Christian religious education and in exaggerated theories of what is distinctively Christian, it has repeatedly been made the point at which creation is negated, and so has been turned into its exact opposite". (p. 95)

What we have here is something that flatly contradicts the use theologians such as Tracey Rowland and the self-proclaimed "postmodern Augustinian Thomists" made of Cardinal Ratzinger's work.

Admittedly he seemed at first to be on the side of the de Lubacians in their suppression of the integrity of the notion of nature (human nature) when endowed with divine grace. The infinite superiority of grace was justly highlighted, as appeared in the Council document *Gaudium et spes*. But de Lubac and his followers fell into the trap described here by Ratzinger himself, which he has picked up in having to deal with the implications for the status of creation as a mighty work also of God.

The gift of the supernatural order does not eliminate that of the natural order. As the pope goes on to say: "The doctrine of creation therefore is inseparably included within the doctrine of redemption. The doctrine of redemption is based on the doctrine of creation, on an irrevocable Yes to creation." (p. 99) … Only if the Redeemer is also Creator can he really be Redeemer (p. 100) So too only if Christ's and our human nature are preserved in their full integrity can he redeem us. This integrity includes that of the natural happiness that is had by reason of being human.

However, the use made of Cardinal Ratzinger's thought generally is matter for a separate treatment. Here we are concerned with his clear teaching on the absolute necessity to keep the doctrine of creation as a philosophical/metaphysical truth that is not to be undermined by any other considerations no matter how exalted.

We will finish off this preface with a summary look at how the five ways can be related to Aristotle's causes. For we are concerned with showing God as the cause of being as we know it, which is necessarily equated with being as created. In order to appreciate this treatment, we must understand that the concept of being (*ens*) though fundamental to human intelligence and thus the simplest of all concepts in our understanding is not to be thought thereby as a simple concrete concept. It is in fact one and undivided but not for that indivisible. For, it is made up of two parts or abstract principles, which are directly related to the fundamental division of being into act and potency. All created being is composed of what it can be (*essentia*) and that whereby it is (*esse*). If one does not keep to this understanding of the whole being one has no hope of following the five ways. As may be evident from what has already been said, no modern scientist of philosopher has any idea in this regard, and it seems few modern theologians.

The five ways can be related to Aristotle's four causes, efficient, final, formal and material, if we appreciate, which we can from analogy with a work of human art, that the formal cause has two modes, one intrinsic and the other extrinsic, which is then called exemplary. The proofs are strictly concerned with establishing an extrinsic cause, of which we clearly have three, efficient, exemplary and final (the second, fourth and fifth ways). The other two ways are taken by reference to the two intrinsic causes, formal and material, but insofar as they are potencies that if they actually exist, suppose an extrinsic act as cause.

The intrinsic formal cause is in fact the basis of the proof from contingency, for it is but essence relative to *esse*. This can best be appreciated by reading Chapter Four of St. Thomas's *De ente et essentia*.

The proof from motion involves matter as potency within the essence for form through which it demands act as extrinsic cause. Thus all are metaphysical proofs if the first way, that from motion, is the more remote intellectually/rationally. St. Thomas says it is the most manifest, which is probably because of the fact that what from which we move is most evident to us. They all however quickly bring the wise to a quasi-immediate conclusion that God as pure act, or *esse,* is the cause of all being as we know it. A perverse "heart", by which one becomes a fool, however, will be an obstacle to admitting anything that is lord over my life and freedom.

Introduction

Our treatment of this subject is divided into three parts; 1) The Existence of God; 2) His Essence; 3) His Attributes. It is based on the works of St. Thomas, in particular his two Summas and his commentaries on Aristotle's Physics and Metaphysics. We acknowledge however a significant dependence upon the work of the Australian Thomist Austin M. Woodbury SM PhD STD in his work on Natural Theology.

The philosophical treatment of God belongs to the philosophy of being or reality considered as a whole, or in all its universality. That is to say it belongs to the study of Metaphysics. This brings into play a serious difficulty for the study of our subject in modern times. For, there has been from the very beginning of the modern era a very definite anti-metaphysical bias in modern education, most operative at the highest level. This anti-intellectual bias directly affects our understanding of the basic notions of truth, goodness and beauty. But it also undermines all objectivity in science and morals and destroys any possibility of a rationally based belief in God and religion.

The fallacy, and even absurdity, of this bias needs to be shown up right at the beginning of the study of Metaphysics and is therefore properly dealt with in the first part, called Epistemology, or Defensive Metaphysics by Dr. Woodbury. However, the bias permeates every aspect of the modern discussion of all issues and we will therefore need to deal with it at each juncture of this course.

For instance, the failure of most "critics" (such as Sir Anthony Kenny) to see the force of the proofs for the existence of God comes from the latent materialism and/or subjectivism that are part of the anti-metaphysical bias in modern science. The very concepts of motion, causality etc. which we use have a subtle materialism, mathematicism or subjectivism inserted into the scientific discussion of them, which even people such as Kenny, supposedly well versed in St. Thomas's thought, unconsciously carry over into the proofs. Materialism is, of course, atheistic; and the mathematics which goes with it in the modern conception of the scientific method, only makes the exclusion of God and the spiritual more complete; but the subjectivism of such as Kant is equally destructive of belief in a real God.

This kind of difficulty we may classify as "extrinsic". There is also much clearing of the ground to be done in any philosophical analysis, with regard to what we may call "intrinsic" difficulties, from the nature of the subject matter itself. There are not only the classical objections to proofs and arguments to be addressed, but also the proper definitions of the problems to be resolved and the kinds of answers to be expected. For instance, not many appreciate the meaning of existence that can apply to our natural or rational knowledge of God. There is more than one meaning of "exist", as Aristotle carefully explains; and we ought not be surprised that the existence to be attributed to God is not to be found anywhere within the whole of creation, whether material or spiritual, let alone that we should expect to find him somewhere in outer space.

Thus, it is not merely because of a cross materialism in our thinking that we mistake the meaning of the question; the ambiguity in the meaning of the notions of being and existence adverted to is a fundamental problem in itself. God's proper act of existence is as

unknowable naturally to any creature as his essence; indeed, this we
know when we conclude that they are identical in reality. We will,
however, come to this aspect of the problem shortly.

The major difficulty however remains that of the anti-
metaphysical assumptions referred to. These are at the bottom of
the peculiar mentality appertaining in modern times that goes by
the general name of "Modernism". A general materialist cast of
mind in the prevailing intellectual and scientific culture is part of
this mentality. But there is much else belonging to a whole range of
presuppositions and assumptions that amount not just to obstacles
in the way of understanding but also cause a veritable mental "road-
block" in the rational discussion of anything about God, or for that
matter about spiritual and religious matters.

Notice that we say the rational discussion of such matters – there
is plenty of non-rational discussion, from a religious standpoint,
and of irrational discussion, from an irreligious standpoint. For,
precisely because of the subtle subjectivism and scepticism underlying all of modern thinking, the arguments of both theists and atheists have much common ground. Even some of those who believe
they are countering modernism are working from its assumptions.

Let us briefly look at what we are entitled to expect in regard to
our knowledge of God from our natural reason. St. Thomas holds
that something can be achieved – but not a lot. He does not treat the
question as a futile one, or one totally above and beyond human
reason. But we might say that he goes as close as one possibly can to
saying that by reason alone we can know nothing about God. There
is no univocal common ground between the creature and the Creator; they are worlds apart, indeed, infinitely, so. We have to be care-

ful in saying for instance that God is a substance or subject. All our
knowledge of God has to be based on what we know about our
world, including ourselves, as it is totally dependent for its existence
upon God. *Non enim possumus nominare Deum nisi ex creaturis, ut*
supra dictum est. Et sic, quidquid dicitur de Deo et creaturis, dicitur
secundum quod est aliquis ordo creaturae ad Deum, ut ad principi-
um et causam, in qua praeexistunt excellenter omnes rerum perfec-
tiones. "For we are not able to name God except from creatures, as
said above. And so, whatever is said about God and creatures, is said
in so far as there is some order of the creature to God, as to a principle or cause, in which pre-exist more excellently all the perfections
of things." (*I, 13, 5 c*) (translation mine)

Being made by God this world has to be like God in some way.
But it is also true to say that there is none like unto God – the unlikeness infinitely surpasses the likeness. We should avoid therefore
trying to treat the comparison or analogy in purely creaturely terms,
as if it were between two things within the order of creation. It is a
question of analogy, but even the analogical basis of the comparison
or connection is unique. It is not like comparing two things according to some common standard; it is rather like trying to compare a
thing with the standard itself according to which it is valued or
measured – and in this unique case the measure transcends the created order of the comparative or relative altogether, with our being
left only with our real dependence upon an ineffable reality.

It is not like comparing two things according to say colour; it is
more like trying to liken a particular colour, say red, to light itself.
In terms of visibility, the colour is in fact more visible to us, and
hence we are more aware of it; but the light is in reality a greater

thing in the order of sight – it is the very reason of visibility, without which nothing would be able to be seen. So, too, universalising this particular comparative effort to two things, the creature and God, according to being itself or existence, it is not like comparing two things that have existence according to beingness or reality, but rather like trying to relate a particular being within our experience (or intellectual vision) to the very source of existence, and the reason of being of everything other than God.

We must be careful, however, not to forget the reality of the relation, which founds our talk about God; so that the existence we assert of God loses all objective reference or real significance. The logical status of the concepts and propositions we form about God are firmly based in the truth of things within our experience and point to a transcendent reality, not to a logical construct.

St. Thomas explains the "is" of our proposition "God therefore exists" is a logical connection that expresses this truth. We have the same sort of trouble in understanding the cause of existence, or the ultimate reason of being as we know it, as we have of "seeing" light - it is manifested to us only in so far as we see coloured things in which the light is activating them. We are reduced to speaking in negative terms, of pure light being "invisible", when what we really want to say is that it is super-visible (taking visibility according to our limited powers of sight).

So, too, God is said to be beyond existence, not to exist so much as to "super-exist". The etymology of the word "exist" points to this: for it literally is derived from *ex sistere*, to stand outside one's causes. So understood God does not exist; he simply and eternally is, uncaused. We have, therefore, as much chance of having an insight into the existence of God as of seeing something perfectly transparent. Yet we are aware of the mysterious presence of God.

This brings us then to consider what we mean when we talk about knowing that God exists, or proving the existence of God. This requires us to resolve the ambiguity in the notions of being and existence already referred to. Aristotle notes that "being" (noun) and "is" (verb) have a primary meaning, as when we refer to a dog as a being, and that it is, from a direct and immediate knowledge of it. Moreover, this notion of being applies to the whole dog, as the thing which exists.

It is a diminished or secondary meaning of being, or (to) exist, that is intended when we refer only to a part or some property or activity of the dog, such as its leg or its bite; these latter do not exist in the primary full sense, even though we may talk about the existence and even the "being" of the leg and of the bite themselves. Change, or become, is another lesser mode of being.

But there is an even more diminished meaning of "being" and "is", noted by Aristotle. It still bears a (causal) connection with the first and full sense; but with it we pass from the order of real existence to the mental or logical. Let us suppose that a young child playing outside is bitten on the leg by a dog. Yet the child is too young to be able to say what happened to him. No one else saw the dog. The doctor identifies the wound as a dog bite and the police go looking for the dog.

Do they know the existence of the dog in the first sense, in its actual existence? No, this they could only know by immediate experience (seeing or hearing etc.) How, then, can they be sure of the real existence of the dog? Only by a process of reasoning from effect to cause (*a posteriori*); real dog bites are caused by existing dogs (if in this kind of case the reasoning is limited to the very time of the bite). The existence of the dog at this stage, therefore, is that of a concluded existence or of an existence in the mind, the existence signified in the proposition: "the dog that bit the child exists". The proposition is true, so we know of the existence of a real dog, but this knowledge is had only by means of reasoning. The proposition intends the real existence of the dog but it does not know it directly.

Much detective work is of this nature, conducted by *a posteriori* reasoning (from effect to proper cause). If the effects are distinctive enough, as in fingerprints, they are sufficient to found a proof of an (existing) individual being as the proper (the one and only) cause. It is not an *a priori* deduction (from cause to effect); but it is a true deduction, not an inductive process. The latter involves the mind reasoning from many things to some one thing or property found to be common in the many. This can lead to sufficient proof but not always.

Certitude of deduction in *a posteriori* reasoning is always had once the existence of the effect, no matter how small (e.g. a fingerprint), is ascertained. The proofs for the existence of God, when properly understood, are put forward as irrefutable. One has greater reason to question the validity of distinctive finger-proof evidence in a court than that of the five ways of St. Thomas.

Now we find that St. Thomas refers to the distinction between knowing God's existence in this way and having the sort of experience where we know the act of existence of the object. He points to Aristotle's distinction between the "is" or being of the proposition, which is a logical relation of union of subject and predicate wholly within the mind, and the actual "is" signified by knowing the act of existence outside the mind, as for instance knowing the dog to be on seeing it. We have to be rather careful here not to think that the being of the proposition does not intend that real existence. For there are two things intended when we predicate something of a subject.

If we say for instance that the dog is blind the "is"does not signify anything of reality in the subject. It simply means to unite a lack of being or privation with the subject. The "is" signifies what is true but not so as to say that there is anything real in the subject. On the other hand, where we say "the dog is running", though in the mind the "is" signifies the union of "running" with the subject it does not mean to leave out something real in the dog. The mode of signification though different from the intention of the statement does not mean to exclude the reality.

It is important to note this subtle combination of logical relation (a second intention) and the reference of the statement (the first intention). Thus on seeing a dog I say "there is a dog": I intend by the "is" the actual existence exercised by the animal. Now when I have not seen the dog but reason to its existence as indicated above I still intend to refer to its real existence. We need to be careful not to reduce the full signification/intention of the "is" of the concluded proposition to a merely logical connection in the mind.

The way that St. Thomas has made the distinction between knowing the real "is" of God and the "is" of the concluded proposition "God exists" can lead one to think that he is saying we do not intend God's real existence. What he is wanting to point out is the difference between knowing directly and indirectly, just as we do not know the dog's real existence in the example given. We intend the real existence of God but we do not have any insight into it except through reasoning to it as a cause. Then all we know about God has to be derived from what can be understood through the effects from which we reason.

This avoids the problem that we cannot know not only the essence but also the existence of God in itself. The same considerations have to be carefully noted when we are speaking about the essence and attributes of God. When we say things like "God is good", "God is wise", though they have to be known with the use of the propositional "is", they are not to be thought of as involving solely a logical relation. Involved also is the intent to refer to something in God but only able to be conceived in terms of creatures. St. Thomas is very clear about this real reference when discussing the attributes of God.

Connected with this intrinsic difficulty in dealing with God's existence and attributes is the extrinsic one, consequential on the anti-metaphysical bias, of the truncated and distorted notion of logic had by the modern mind. The probative force of deduction is denied, reduced to tautology; the distinction between *a posteriori* reasoning and induction is not understood; all rational process of any value in empirical science is reduced to a weak notion of "induction". All this obfuscation is the necessary background to the radically sceptical mind. The proofs of the existence of God (as are all logical proofs) are regarded as refutable in principle; no need to go through the motions.

This bias against general logic, or the universal application of our reason, is most subtle; for it involves a pretence that the metaphysical conclusions that follow necessarily from facts obvious to sense somehow offend "scientific method". This limitation put upon rational method is dictated by the anti-metaphysical bias; it is a particularist method that corresponds to a particularist philosophy, an empirico-mathematical method that matches up with an order of knowledge in which Mathematics is regarded as the supreme science.

Thus, not only is the full object of our intellectual understanding of reality arbitrarily constricted to the world of matter and quantity, so is the range of our reasoning similarly restricted, not to speak of the degradation of the mode of reasoning itself. What we have to contend with, then, is a bias against both the Metaphysics and Logic of Aristotle, which properly appreciated are only the elaboration of our basic common sense grasp of reality and our natural power of reasoning.

The proofs for the existence of God conclude to a knowledge of the existence of a cause unknown as to its proper nature, but only knowable by analogy through creatures, and that of a special kind. God shares nothing even in the order of essence with creatures. For essence names a potency to exist according to some limited form of being. God's existence and "nature" transcend the whole essential order and therefore the intellectual ability of all created intellects. Both the existence and essence of God are unintelligible to us (because super-intelligible), just as pure light is invisible. All that is possible is a dim realisation derived from the fact that we do share some sort of existence with our Creator.

So what name can we give this superlative being? Just as we know him indirectly so we can only name him indirectly. Having identified the cause of the effects in five ways St. Thomas simply says:

"and this is what everyone understands by the name 'God'. The various names of God in different languages, "uncaused cause", "almighty", "omniscient", "all good", show how they come from phenomena in creation. The names of "God", such as almighty, all wise, all good, even pure Act or existence itself (*esse*), though they are, as understood by us, totally inadequate to the reality, are not for that meaningless. The realities are necessarily taken by us from creatures and exist in God, but in a manner that we cannot comprehend.

The paradox of our knowledge of God being rather of what he is not than what he is will be taken up more fully when we come to examine the essence and attributes of God. If we keep these clarifications given above in mind we are better placed to proceed with the examination of the rational proofs for the existence of God.

Existence of God – Preliminary Considerations

There are two preliminary questions that need to be addressed before we can proceed with the proofs. The first is: Is it necessary to have a proof for the existence of God? For, there are those who say that such existence is self-evident. The second question is: Is it possible to prove by reason that there is a God? For, there are some, indeed, many today, who say that there is no way of proving that there is a God.

The two questions are not always addressed, especially in modern philosophy. For the notion of proof itself is not distinctly understood, and again "proof" is not clearly confined to the order of knowledge. Take Kant's philosophy, for instance. He says that it is not possible to know by theoretical reason anything beyond the sensible "empirical" world, and even that is not known as something real (thing-in-itself). So, by such arbitrary limitation of the object of our intellectual knowledge, he excludes any possibility of proof as generally understood by all thinkers before him, and by common sense. But then, he says that such "theoretical" or "scientific" proof is not necessary – for the existence of God is demanded by our practical need or desire for good. There is, if you like, a moral proof, which founds our belief in God.

The problem with this peculiar mental stance is that the (practical) order of action depends for its very existence upon the (theoretical) order of knowledge (the will is in the reason or intellect). Will is an inclination for good known intellectually or understood. One does not, cannot, will or desire the totally unknown. So Kant, in separating the practical from the theoretical order, having destroyed the objectivity of the latter, has effectively destroyed the objective value of the former. The moral proof, based upon desire, can have no force and indeed makes no sense without the rational proof based on knowledge.

Kant's philosophy is the father of all modern pragmatism, which is a subtle variant of the irrationalism that underlies the various forms of modernist thinking. Apart from the religious modernists, most others simply take the skeptical basis of philosophy as destroying any possibility of belief in a God, which even for Kant amounts to a reliance upon blind "faith". Given the agnosticism built into his theoretical philosophy all Kant's criticisms of the theoretical or philosophical proofs for the existence of God are quite gratuitous. They amount to simply reiterating the bare assertion that we can have no objective basis for belief in anything. Yet there is hardly a modern thinker, including many a Catholic one, who is not taken in by this.

But, let us attempt to deal with the first preliminary question by itself: Is the existence of God self-evident? Even here we have to contend with a fairly common confusion about the meaning of "self-evident". Strictly speaking, it means that no proof is needed; but often it is equated with what is known by means of an *a priori* proof. Take St. Anselm's "ontological" proof, for instance. It is generally regarded as a case of a proof of the existence *a priori*, in the following form: That which nothing greater can be conceived must include actual existence. God is that which nothing greater can be conceived. Therefore God exists.

But, put in another form, it is simply asserted that God cannot be thought of without existence, or as necessarily existing, and therefore that God exists is self-evident. St. Thomas in fact deals with it in answer to an objection under the question: "Whether the existence of God is self-evident?" St. Thomas does not deny that existence is necessarily contained in the concept of God, or that the proposition "God exists" is known as soon as the terms "God" and "existence" are known, and so is formally a self-evident proposition. But he denies that it is actual existence which is thereby understood. Existence itself is an abstract concept whereby we endeavour to conceive it apart from essence. Cajetan, noting this, famously said: "Existence does not exist". The fact that we can conceive something does not prove it exists in the concrete. To do this we need to start with what does actually exist.

The necessary link between God and existence is made in the mind only; for a proposition to refer to actual or real existence there has to be a direct connection (from sense experience or intellectual consciousness) or at least an indirect connection (from reasoning) with what actually exists. The "smuggling in" of actual existence into the wholly internal mental process involved makes it look as if some conclusion is arrived at, as in the form of the syllogism above.

St. Thomas deals with two other objections in relation to the question whether the existence of God is self-evident. The first is to do with the natural desire for happiness, which in fact and truth is God. Now we do not desire anything unless we first know it. Hence we must know that God exists. The answer to this is that God is only known in a general and confused way, not distinctly or absolutely. What we naturally desire is happiness in general, without knowing at first in what happiness really consists, even though we can readily conclude (by reasoning) to God being that in which our true happiness lies. Some so clearly and easily make this rational connection that it seems that they understand immediately that God exists.

The other objection has to do with the self evidence of the existence of truth to us; God is truth, so his existence too must be self evident. The same sort of answer applies: "The existence of truth in general is self evident but the existence of a First Truth is not self evident to us". In his general response to the question St. Thomas notes a distinction between what may be self evident "in itself" and what is self-evident "to us". In many cases these two coincide. That a whole is greater than any of its parts is self evident both in itself and to us. So too is any definition of a thing which is clearly understood: that a triangle is a three sided figure is self evident in itself and to anyone who understands what a triangle is. But of things the natures of which we do not fully understand it is possible that what is self evident in itself is not self evident to us. Thus, not everyone understands the meaning of a purely spiritual being, i.e. an angel. That the angel does not occupy any physical space is clear from its very definition; so such a proposition is self evident in itself; but what it asserts may not be self evident to one who does not have a clear idea of what angel means.

St. Thomas applies this distinction to our knowledge of God. It can be true that the proposition "God exists" is self evident in itself, and indeed in logical terms this is so, in that our concept of God in the mind necessarily includes existence. But no one naturally has any knowledge of God's essence in real terms (only available in the vision of God), so the real identification is not self evident to us. This means that we need to prove God's existence (as necessary cause) from the existence of his effects.

This brings us to the second question: Is it possible to prove by reason that there is a God? St. Thomas deals with three objections (in other more specialised works he deals with many more but in the Summa he usually selects only two or three of the strongest). The first is not strictly relevant to Natural Theology but only to Sacred Theology: that what is known by divine faith cannot be proved from reason (or demonstrated). But that God exists is known by Faith. St. Thomas's answer is that the existence of God is not strictly speaking an article of faith but a preamble to the articles – so it requires a natural demonstration. There is also the fact that some things revealed are but confirmations of what we can know naturally, such as the Ten Commandments.

There is nothing to prevent someone who cannot see the proof from believing it on Faith (which is a higher and more certain way –

without denying the necessity for the rational conclusion). Nor, though St. Thomas does not say it here, would it seem to prevent a person having two "motives" for belief, one natural and one supernatural, at least if the two notions of God are quite different.

The other two objections address the issue more directly, and their answers both involve the distinction between *a priori* and *a posteriori* proof or demonstration. Rational proof requires something being asserted of a subject; but that requires a prior knowledge of the subject, and indeed of the nature or essence of the subject. This is quite obvious in a priori proof for it proceeds from a knowledge of the essence, as the conclusions about triangles flow from a distinct knowledge of what a triangle is. But it also holds with a posteriori proof. What we have to rely upon here, however, is the meaning of the name we use to refer to the subject. Being only known as a cause, this meaning has to be taken from effects; it is not a knowledge of the essence of itself but through its effects, as appears before in our example of the police's indirect understanding of what they are looking for. St. Thomas answers the second objection in this way.

The third objection raises the problem of the infinite distance between God and his effects, a problem unique to the case of God. As St. Thomas answers, this improportion points to the inadequacy of our knowledge of the cause, not to an impossibility of knowing of the existence of the cause; we have the least perfect knowledge of God, but "from every effect the existence of the cause can be clearly demonstrated".

So we have cleared the way to the proofs for the existence of God. It is evident that these proofs can only be from effect to cause, *a pos-*

teriori. By disconnecting our intellect and reason from the real world modern philosophy has undermined this way to God. Accordingly, modern thinkers fail to appreciate the difference between *a priori* and *a posteriori* reasoning and become occupied with analysing and refuting arguments of an *a priori* kind (such as the "ontological proof"). In fact, *a priori* reasoning becomes virtually confined to mathematical proof, and approaches the status of self evidence; whilst *a posteriori* proof is virtually reduced to inductive reasoning, and regarded as unable to issue in certainty.

Kant, indeed, completed the closure of the modern mind in this regard by redefining "a priori" and "a posteriori", so that they are divorced for any deductive reasoning at all. For, he transferred the terms from the order of reasoning to the order of judgment. For Aristotle reasoning or proof is only required when things (or propositions regarding them) are not self evident, or immediately known. One does not need to prove that snow is white, or that one should honour one's parents. If the former is not evident to a person of sound mind he should have his eyesight checked; if one does not hold to the latter, Aristotle says, he requires not argument but reprimand.

For Kant, the action of theoretical Reason, or Understanding (Verstand), is not a matter of coming to a conclusion, but of applying an a priori form to an empirical matter, much after the fashion that the artist applies his ideas to materials – even the "form" of causality (the very basis of reasoning) is thought of in this way. Kant spends the whole of his time in this regard working out what these ideas or a priori forms are, as if he were the architect of the universe. The function of a posteriori reason, to his mind, is to note the regularity in what empirically happens, a sort of weak induction. He thus prepared the ground for the later treatment of logic and science as concerned with tautologies and hypothetical propositions.

But we need not enter here into this crazy world of inconsequence and arbitrary assertions except to note that it underpins all modern disdain for the proofs for the existence of God. There is still work to be done without being so side-tracked. For, before we present the arguments for the existence of God we need to say something about the two most principal objections to the proofs which, though addressed and answered long ago by St. Thomas, have again been raised in rather strident form in recent times, and most loudly, to much acclaim by a brain-washed populace, by a biological scientist (Dawkins) and a journalist (Hitchins).

We will come back to the particular arguments of these modern atheists, but let us here look at the objections themselves in their classical form, precisely as put by St. Thomas: "(1). It seems that God does not exist; because if one of two contraries be infinite, the other would be altogether destroyed. But the word 'God' means that He is infinite goodness. If, therefore, God existed, there would be no evil discoverable; but there is evil in the world. Therefore God does not exist.

(2). Further, it is superfluous to suppose that what can be accounted for by a few principles has been produced by many. But it seems that everything we see in the world can be accounted for by other principles, supposing God did not exist. For all natural things can be reduced to one principle which is nature; and all voluntary things can be reduced to one principle which is human reason, or will. Therefore there is no need to suppose God's existence."

The first objection, therefore, is from the existence of evil, and argues to the incompatibility of this with a good God; the second is from the fact that all things and events can be explained by natural science, and anything beyond that by reference to human intelligence and will, and it therefore argues that an appeal to the causality of God is unnecessary and gratuitous.

The first objection has force only if the evil which we know from our experience is understood as necessarily opposed to the goodness of God. So the answer to the objection does not have to rely upon denying the reality of evil, or of downplaying its significance. There is no great point therefore in efforts of many to overwhelm us with the magnitude of evil in the world. If God can use evil in some way in the production of good then the goodness of God is not denied or diminished by the presence of evil, no matter how great. The most expert of artists, take Rembrandt for instance, make use not only of light and colour but also of darkness and shade to produce an effect that cannot be had without them – to highlight by contrast – so perhaps there is some point to the presence of evil in God's work.

In any case one cannot deny the artist's right to use all the contrasts available, provided they are artistically ordered to the brilliant beauty of the whole work. It is a poor art critic, or one with a particular reason to denigrate the artist, who looks at the parts of a painting in isolation, or according to a partial perspective, in order to find fault with it.

St. Augustine answers the objection in his Enchridion, which St. Thomas quotes in his answer: *Deus, cum sit summe bonus, nullo modo sineret aliquid mali esse in operibus suis, nisi esset adeo omnipotens et bonus, ut bene faceret etiam de malo.* "God, since he is the summit of goodness, in no way would have allowed evil to be in his works, unless he were all powerful and good to such an extent that even from evil he bring forth good." (translation mine)

Such a use of evil by no means contradicts the goodness of God; rather does it point to an even greater goodness in God, just as Rembrandt's art is shown to be greater because of his ability to use not only light and colour but also darkness and shade. A closer analysis of the meaning of evil will also show that it does not really contradict goodness, but in fact supposes it. It has no power from itself but relies for all its force upon the good in which it is a lack of due good.

St Thomas answers the second objection by pointing to the changeability and defectibility of all created things whether material or spiritual. All material activity involves movement or change, and is liable to "run down" over time; the fire which naturally is the cause of heat in other things is itself not pure heat but needs to be continually refuelled. Living things which are the natural causes of vital activity are not purely or perfectly self-acting. In the spiritual order, where will seems to be the ultimate cause of activity, and seemingly able to be "motiveless", will can fail to achieve its object; no created will is infallibly in control of itself or others. This changeability and defectibility comes from the very nature of all created things – from the fact that they are based in potentialities which need to be actualized and directed from outside themselves, and ultimately from an unchanging and indefectible cause, as St. Thomas argues: "for all things that are changeable and capable of defect must be traced back to an immovable and self-necessary first principle, as was shown in the body of the Article."

This second objection, however, needs some closer examination in view of the anti-metaphysical bias of modern thought noted. It is particularly necessary in respect of the first and second ways, with the modern scientific mind not accustomed to rise above the levels of natural science and mathematics. There is a shift in St. Thomas's presentation of the argument from the material level of being to the spiritual when he answers the objection so far as it relates to the will. For here we have something and its activity that is spiritual. This needs to be addressed specially since its change is not motion strictly taken.

This shift comes out in Aristotle's use of the proof from motion against the background of having to appeal to a spiritual realm in order to account for the "eternal" nature of motion and time that he posits. For, as he argues, motion itself (and hence time) is an intermediate kind of action where it can only be understood of something that has been moved and will be moved. If it has not been moved the motion has not begun; if it will not be moved the motion has ceased. So the origin and termination of motion cannot be accounted for within motion itself.

The principle of motion is that whatever is in motion has been moved by another and if that has been moved to move then it too is moved by another and so on ad infinitum. There is a certain (potential) infinity in the very act of motion. But then there is the other principle that if there is no first mover then the motion cannot have begun. Thus we have to posit a moving principle/cause outside the order of motion. That leads Aristotle to posit the action of an immaterial thing or separated substance, or spiritual being. Then Aristotle notes that if this spiritual being is such that it is potential to its activity, it too needs an extrinsic "mover". The dependence has to terminate at a being that is pure act that is necessarily one only, which is the notion of God.

St. Thomas notes the supposition of the eternity of motion (and time) used by Aristotle in the proof but denies that it is demonstratively valid. Nonetheless, the conclusion arrived at of the existence of God is not thereby undermined. For, it is even more evident if motion has a beginning. Such beginning, however, cannot be in time: it must be outside or rather above time. Thinking of time before this is a work of our imagination (where the mathematician lives).

Both Aristotle and St. Thomas rely on a physical state of affairs as the factual basis for the proof. But then they rely on a metaphysical distinction to provide the principle that will carry the argument to the end. This is so even in the proof as presented in the Physics. That is the distinction between act and potency, taken as applicable to our very understanding of being. That means that we must "move" beyond its application to physical motions and take it in all its universal application beyond its physical manifestation. This proceeding belongs to all five ways.

We must note however that Aristotle uses "eternal" in more than one sense. Applied to the duration of motion and time it means no more than lacking beginning or end. This is a notion of infinity that derives from matter and signifies potential infinity. The proper notion of eternal is what is actually infinite and only applies to God as pure act. In between we have a third notion, called more properly *aevum*.

Thus, there is an initial shift in the argument from motion from material being to spiritual being, so that separated substances may be conceived as moving bodily natures, without themselves being moved in the strictest sense. Motion in regard has to be taken analogously. We should also note that Aristotle concludes that the spiritual order of things has to be understood in terms of intellect and will.

This shift is already made by St. Thomas when he applies the argument to the human will. St. Thomas will point to its changeability so that it looks as if it has the defectibility of physical movents. But this sort of potentiality does not belong essentially to the will. The will is a spiritual power, and hence a spiritual mover that does not change materially. Such kind of defectibility comes from accompanying bodily processes. To grasp the full force of the proof we have to appreciate that even our free will has to be moved ultimately by God, because metaphysically it too has to move from potency to act.

Indeed, we may suspect that the failure to attribute necessity to the proofs derives in an important respect from human pride; to the fact that in regard to our human actions we do not see the need to go beyond the act of our will. There is nothing "forcing" me to do anything I do not choose to do. There may be a material necessity in things below, which one's materialism may allow. Over these we exercise some degree of dominance. But no necessity is felt with regard to things above. The materialist and the atheist of course cannot account for his feeling of such (spiritual) freedom but holds his contradictory attitude for reasons of morality or rather immorality (quasi-religiously).

The kind of unmoved motor thus has to be refined on the way to the existence of God. There is the first shift where we know that causation of material motion is to be distinguished clearly from that proceeding from will, a spiritual principle of motion even in our own experience. The second objection, however, overlooks the fact that the natural explanations of physical science and the efficacy of human action are both secondary movents, needing to proceed to action from a situation of potentiality. Human reason and will, too, cannot be first movents, despite the great superiority they have over physical movents.

These considerations come into play in all the five ways, which are so succinctly outlined by St. Thomas that they may look as if jumping to their conclusions. They all come down to recognising that though taken from physical facts they are subjected to meta-physical principles. Ultimately, therefore, they are metaphysical proofs, even where dealt with in the Physics. Aristotle evidently brings the proof from motion in there to complete the explanation of physical reality. But let us now proceed to consider the proofs themselves as presented by St. Thomas.

Postscript

Before proceeding we should mention a curious aspect to Aristo-tle's consideration in Book 12 of the Metaphysics where in attempt-ing to explain how a first mover can be unmoved when exercising influence on what is moved. Aristotle necessarily thought of God as creator when he described him as the unmoved mover. For every natural created thing is a moved mover. But then he tried to explain how God could be unmoved and proposed that this could only be of something that "moves" by being the object of knowledge and desire. That is to say in so far as it is an object of intelligence and love, an intelligible and desirable object.

This led to his conclusion in Book 12 of the Metaphysics that God moved everything else as a ruler does, without himself being moved. But it was a rule by a supreme intellect and will, that in fact was not just an understander but an act of understanding, the understand of an understand. In terms of potency and act God had to be entirely without potency, i.e. pure act.

This poses a problem for us in that we cannot move things not under our control by simply willing them to happen, that is, as being mere objects of desire. Where does the will of the ruler get its efficiency from? What is a legislator to do in expressing its will without an executive that exercises the necessary force? This force attaches to the motion of creatures without any necessary connection with intelligence or will, or in us with intelligence and will at the lowest level of life and being. It seems to be intrinsically connected with moved movers. How can we communicate the efficiency of the efficient cause at the level of knowledge and desire alone?

The answer has to be that in the case of God everything created is under his control so he can effect things by sheer will power. We have some notion of this in seeing that the higher levels of being contain the perfections of the lower. So there has to be the power to do in them what is in the power of the lower, such as to move things locally. There is then I believe a bit of a gap to be filled in Aristotle's explanation though it would have to be there implicitly. We are accustomed to associate force and efficient causality with the region of reality below knowledge and desire. But animals are superior to things below even in terms of power as well as sense knowledge and appetite. It is just that the brute's force is elicited by desire directed by knowledge. Relatively to intellectual desire (will) directed by reason it is called brute force but then it means without the proper direction of reason.

Now we know that God's power is supreme even in terms of efficient causality but we do not always associate it with intellect and will or the exercise of intelligence and love, precisely because God's power is above our understanding, and we generally equate efficient causality with force devoid of intelligence and will. Former pope Benedict XVI showed how this is to misunderstand the relation between God's power reason and will.

We distinguish God's absolute power from his ordinate power. But that can only be a logical consideration that is not reflected in God's real being or essence. For God's exercise of his power is necessarily one with that of his intelligence and love. And the creature's relation to God is as an object not just of knowledge and love but also of his power to move, without being moved himself. The first two ways of proving the existence of God, from motion and causality in creatures, are in respect of being subject to this efficient or moving power. The last two relate more directly to his intelligence and will. The third relates to the nature of his existence.

But we can safely assume that Aristotle held at least implicitly to the fact of God as creator. When St. Thomas is discussing the proof of the existence of God he makes the point that it is harder to see creation if the world is held to be eternal but Aristotle has in fact argued from there to the existence of a first unmoved mover.

Part 1

The Existence of God

Chapter 1

Existence of God – The First Way

Prima autem et manifestior via est, quae sumitur ex parte motus. Certum est enim, et sensu constat, aliqua moveri in hoc mundo. Omne autem quod movetur, ab alio movetur. Nihil enim movetur, nisi secundum quod est in potentia ad illud ad quod movetur, movet autem aliquid secundum quod est actu. Movere enim nihil aliud est quam educere aliquid de potentia in actum, de potentia autem non potest aliquid reduci in actum, nisi per aliquod ens in actu, sicut calidum in actu, ut ignis, facit lignum, quod est calidum in potentia, esse actu calidum, et per hoc movet et alterat ipsum. Non autem est possibile ut idem sit simul in actu et potentia secundum idem, sed solum secundum diversa, quod enim est calidum in actu, non potest simul esse calidum in potentia, sed est simul frigidum in potentia. Impossibile est ergo quod, secundum idem et eodem modo, aliquid sit movens et motum, vel quod moveat seipsum. Omne ergo quod movetur, oportet ab alio moveri. Si ergo id a quo movetur, moveatur, oportet et ipsum ab alio moveri et illud ab alio. Hic autem non est procedere in infinitum, quia sic non esset aliquod primum movens; et per consequens nec aliquod aliud movens, quia moventia secunda non movent nisi per hoc quod sunt mota a primo movente, sicut baculus non movet nisi per hoc quod est motus a manu. Ergo necesse est devenire ad aliquod primum movens, quod a nullo movetur, et hoc omnes intelligunt Deum.

"The first and more manifest way is the argument from motion. It is certain, and evident to our senses, that in the world some things are in motion. Now whatever is in motion is put in motion by another, for nothing can be in motion except it is in potentiality to that towards which it is in motion; whereas a thing moves inasmuch as it is in act. For, motion is nothing else than the reduction of something from potentiality to actuality. But nothing can be reduced from potentiality to actuality, except by something in a state of actuality. Thus that which is actually hot, as fire, makes wood, which is potentially hot, to be actually hot, and thereby moves and changes it. Now it is not possible that the same thing should be at once in actuality and potentiality in the same respect, but only in different respects. For what is actually hot cannot simultaneously be potentially hot; but it is simultaneously potentially cold. It is therefore impossible that in the same respect and in the same way a thing should be both mover and moved, i.e. that it should move itself. Therefore, whatever is in motion must be put in motion by another. If that by which it is put in motion be itself put in motion, then this also must needs be put in motion by another, and that by another again. But this cannot go on to infinity, because then there would be no first mover, and, consequently, no other mover; seeing that subsequent movers move only inasmuch as they are put in motion by the first mover; as the staff moves only because it is put in motion by the hand. Therefore it is necessary to arrive at a first mover, put in motion by no other; and this everyone understands to be God."

The above is St. Thomas's exposition of the first proof or demonstration that God exists. As already noted any such proof has to be an a posteriori one (from effect to cause). Hence, it starts with the fact that the effect exists. In this case the effect is "motion". There are particular problems with the modern understanding of this notion and its difference from that of Aristotle and St. Thomas that we will come to shortly. But let us examine more closely the argument of St. Thomas. Firstly, he relies on the fact that "motion is nothing other than the reduction of something from potentiality to actuality". The latin *movere enim nihil aliud quameducere aliquid de potentia in actum* is better translated in concrete terms "for to move is nothing other than to draw out something from potency into act". Part of the problem with dealing with these proofs in English translation is the tendency to use abstract terms for concrete ones. This already removes one from the impact of the concrete.

Furthermore, there is a linguistic confusion that muddles one's thinking. "Motion" as such abstracts from "to move" and "to be moved". Indeed, when we say something is "in motion" we are employing what is called the middle voice, which presupposes the active voice and the passive voice, but which allows us to consider the motion by itself. This voice is separately treated in Greek but other languages use the active or the passive to serve for the middle. Thus Latin uses the passive and English the active and we have to look to the context to identify it as distinct. Hence, in English we say: "the butter cuts well". This is a use of the active voice for the middle. In Latin it is said: "whatever is moved is moved by another", which can simply mean whatever is in motion is moved by some agent. The use of the passive voice for the middle makes it look as if we are voicing a tautology. In English we would prefer to say: "whatever moves is moved by another". The thing is that the "effect" we mean to bring out is simply the motion or movement. In reality this is equivalent to the action from the agent (mover) and to the passion in the patient (moved), as for instance in heating the agent is the fire and the patient is the water.

The important thing to note is that the motion is of and in the patient. That is where the change occurs. Though there may be change in the agent this is not necessarily so, which comes out more clearly when we are dealing with the second way. Intermediate movements are where the motion is from an agent, which itself is a patient from what comes before, and a patient that is itself an agent from what follows. The force of the proof rests on the understanding that there can be an agent that is not a patient, and therefore a first mover/unmoved and a patient that is not an agent, and therefore is a last effect. An agent therefore does not necessarily suppose it being moved. But any effect supposes a moving on the part of some agent. Yet, when we say: "whatever moves is moved by another" we are confused because of the possible ambiguity, tending to take what is a middle voice for an active.

In Latin there is not such a ground for confusion. For the passive necessarily implies the active. But the active implies the passive only where there is change by way of motion. Aristotle had already noted that the two accidents of action and passion that apply to the physical world are but the same movement considered in two ways, as coming from an agent, and as in a patient.

The "abstraction" seen in the use of the middle voice is further reinforced in the modern mind by the identification of science with mathematical physics. Mathematics does not have motion in its object but physical science does. The two are combined to produce a medial science that is formally mathematical and materially physical. That way motion is subjected to mathematical analysis as if it were in some way immobile (at rest). It is treated as if it need not involve change or the action of an external agent to account for its motion. This is particularly envisaged in the case of local motion.

Relying on Newton's first law, Anthony Kenny asks: "Why cannot there be simply motion without an external force?" Such an objection arises from a mistaking of a mathematical abstraction for the real. But local motion means change of place. So the body in local motion is continually changing. That can only be measured by reference to the difference in place, not necessarily in the change in the motion of the body if it is considered in terms of constant speed. Because he was concerned with celestial bodies, which are naturally in motion and apparently moving at a constant speed Newton considered them as self-moving at the same speed, treating them the same as a body at rest. He was interested in the external forces that influenced the speed and direction of the moving body.

But pure physically considered one still has to account for the motion even though it is naturally constant and apparently internal. From the argument of Aristotle this apparent self-movement cannot be the answer, as he showed in the case of living bodies. So one does not escape the necessity of a prior mover that is a first unmoved mover. All this is outside the physico-mathematical interest of the Newtonian scientist, for it is ultimately a metaphysical question.

Kenny goes on to conclude: "It seems that Newton's law wrecks the argument of the first way. For at any given time the rectilinear uniform motion of a body can be explained by the principle of inertia in terms of the body's own previous motion without appeal to any other agent." ("The Five Ways: Saint Thomas Aquinas' Proofs of God's Existence", Uni. of Notre Dame Press, Notre Dame Indiana, 1980, p. 28) The Newtonian principle of inertia is from only a partial mathematicized viewpoint. It is not pure physics but mathematical physics, as plainly appears from the very title of Newton's famous work, *Principia Mathematica Philosophiae Naturalis* ("Mathematical Principles of Natural Philosophy").

Wherever there is quantity in the physical world there is a basis for mathematical analysis, not just pure mathematics but also physico-mathematics. Since Newton this mixed science has come to dominate modern scientific thinking. This has not changed essentially in the new physics of Einstein and Planck, who have adjusted it to the improved observations at the macro and micro levels, thus moderating its absolutist and deterministic conclusions. Because quantity however is so intimate to physical reality physico-mathematics has entered into practically every natural science from the lowest mineral level to the highest animal level of human bodily existence. Moreover, the mathematical side of this (theoretical) scientific approach has come more and more to dominate every field, even the (practical) social economic and political.

Though this has produced much material success in the control of natural forces for the benefit of humanity, more and more at the expense of the natural environment, its inherent materialism and atheism has led humanity down the path of social degradation and moral depravity, with the Catholic Church seen as the main enemy. We might only note that this does not apply only to the political "socialist democracies" but also to the "liberal(ist) democracies". For modern science is underpinned by the liberalist ideology which in the politico-economic sphere has split into two opposed sub-ideologies of Communism and Capitalism.

However, we are primarily concerned here with the modern scientific understanding of motion. Because it is focused on quantity and measurement modern science tends to reduce everything to local motion, whereas Aristotle identified two other distinct kinds of motion, change of quality in alteration and change of quantity in growth, and even mutation, as change of material substance in generation and corruption. The activity presupposed is reduced in modern thought to a concept of energy that is the lowest kind of activity and within the natural elements found to most powerful indeed.

So it is proposed that material reality, and hence all reality, is "nothing but" some sort of "mass" itself reducible to microscopic particles and "energy" divided into potential and kinetic, found in gravitation, electromagnetism, strong and weak nuclear forces. A unified explanation of force so conceived has not yet been produced. Moreover the motion of the particles is thought to be of a wave nature in order to explain certain phenomena occurring in experiments.

But none of this affects the metaphysical implications of motion seen in terms of the transition from potency to act. As Maritain said, one only needs to observe a leaf falling from a tree to bring in the notion of motion from which one is led to conclude the existence of an agency that is not moved to move the motion in a body but does so as a first unmoved mover. That requires us to go outside the series of moved movers that characterise the activity of material nature (and analogously of all created being).

Then the implications of the actuality of such an absolutely un-moved mover takes us to pure activity. Thus we have the notion of pure act, absolutely without potency or change of any kind. This requires an agent that originates the movement of all things in which there is motion and in which things there must be some prin-ciple of potency from which any change to a new form or act has to be educed.

St. Thomas claims this is the more manifest proof. But that ap-plies to one whose grasp of metaphysical principles is not excluded or obscured. The modern mind, immersed in the study of the mate-rial world, not disposed to go outside the considerations of natural science and mathematics, does not adequately see even this world according to its full reality; and is content, deliberately or otherwise, to deny the existence of its creator and treat metaphysical distinc-tions and implications as "unscientific". The force of this prejudice can be seen in someone like Anthony Kenny, whose studies for the priesthood and even of St. Thomas did not prove sufficient to resist the anti-metaphysical implications of subjecting our knowledge of the world to the limitations of the empirical and the mathematical objects of modern science.

One thing to notice is that the first mover (or primary movent) does not necessarily have to be agent that has actually the quality, quantity or locomotion that arises from its action in a body to be the cause of its motion or mutation. It needs to be only a superior be-ing, having the active power to produce the effect. A builder does not need to have the form of a house to produce one, though that form has to be within him is some way, in his intellect. Similarly, the ultimate source of heat does not need to be hot, but can bring what is understood as heat into existence.

So we deduce the cause of motion to something that is without motion, a cause of physical change that is not in a process of change itself. Why, then, should we not stop at a spiritual or non-material being, which need not be God? Let us suppose, then, that all earthly or physical motion can be traced to spiritual powers or angels or pure spirits. We have reached a source of motion, which is not itself in motion in the strict sense. Do we need to go further?

The fact is that though we can from our intellect understand somewhat the nature of separated substances we cannot apodictically prove the existence of created spiritual beings (other than our own spiritual soul) because we only know them in idea. The proof of the existence of God does not depend on our having an idea of God, as Anselm and Descartes thought. Plato made this mistake in regard to his theory of the existence of Forms or Ideas. We have to move from effects that are existing outside our understanding and which demand a cause that can account for their existence. That is the way of Aristotle and St. Thomas.

The modern understanding of motion has two aspects. The first is that the primary scientific consideration of motion (and time) is mathematical. The second is that the physical side of this science is reductionist. This means that it tends to a materialist and empiricist analysis of physical phenomena. In regard to motion this means that all physical change is explained in terms of local motion. This of itself does not affect the validity of the proof. But change of place is the most tenuous of changes. It had of course much greater significance in ancient physics but, in the modern understanding, change of position or place does not seem to make any real difference to things. The whole process might very well be treated as entirely accidental and there seems to be no need for an external mover.

But, though this accidental character attributed to motion is an influence in the matter, the major difference and difficulty for the proof is in the mathematical abstraction applied to the notion of motion itself. The concept already abstracts from a beginning and an end. It names the process in the middle. But in reality it demands a beginning and an end, as it does an agent or mover and a subject or receiver. Physical movement or any change necessarily involves an action on the part of some thing coupled with a "passion" (reception) on the part of another. From the side of the former, motion is an action; from the side of the latter, it is a passion. Heating may be considered in itself but it is the same as the action of the fire and the passion of the water taken from different standpoints.

Mathematically considered, however, this abstraction from physical agents and material subjects is a part of the notion of motion. For, the treatment is purely formal, of the "form", without consideration of physical agencies, subjects or ends. Mathematics abstracts from extrinsic causes; but no more denies the existence of the rectangular shape in a table, nor asserts that it exists without physical change. The form considered is looked at purely in quantitative terms, or according as it is measurable. In this mathematical analysis there is no reason, then, to bring in anything to account for the beginning of the movement or its end. So far as this kind of scientific analysis is concerned, the motion itself is "frozen"; it may be treated as unchanging. This, of course, denies the very nature of physical change, but the mathematician is not interested in this. Any physical adjustments are external to his science.

Modern science is generally reduced to a physico-mathematical consideration of things, which means that it is formally mathematical and materially physical. This is a valid science and its methodology is a valid one, but unfortunately it has come to be regarded as the only scientific method. This has resulted in motion being considered purely from a formal mathematical viewpoint. So pervasive, however, is the fascination with mathematics in modern thinking that the objections made by such as Kenny are thought to have great force.

This domination by mathematics of the modern mind (since Descartes) may also explain the tendency of religiously minded thinkers to want to find an *a priori* proof for the existence of God, as this is the only notion of certain or demonstrative proof that they have. This way, however, as St. Thomas had already noted, is a dead-end, as it depends upon a purported understanding of the nature of God, which is impossible to have by our natural reason.

Many if not most modern-day Catholics, whose education is hugely influenced by this anti-metaphysical bias within the secular education system of the West, are accordingly unable to distinguish between the nature of motion as evident even to common sense and that considered purely as a mathematically abstract form imposed upon a naturally formless matter. They struggle to understand the quite straightforward *a posteriori* proof of St. Thomas, let alone to defend it.

The second way, to which we now turn, is similar to the first but its starting point is distinct, being not motion itself but the passive-active causality that belongs to natural (and all created) agents.

Chapter 2

Existence of God – The Second Way

Secunda via est ex ratione causae efficientis. Invenimus enim in istis sensibilibus esse ordinem causarum efficientium, nec tamen invenitur, nec est possibile, quod aliquid sit causa efficiens sui ipsius; quia sic esset prius seipso, quod est impossibile. Non autem est possibile quod in causis efficientibus procedatur in infinitum. Quia in omnibus causis efficientibus ordinatis, primum est causa medii, et medium est causa ultimi, sive media sint plura sive unum tantum, remota autem causa, removetur effectus, ergo, si non fuerit primum in causis efficientibus, non erit ultimum nec medium. Sed si procedatur in infinitum in causis efficientibus, non erit prima causa efficiens, et sic non erit nec effectus ultimus, nec causae efficientes mediae, quod patet esse falsum. Ergo est necesse ponere aliquam causam efficientem primam, quam omnes Deum nominant.

"The second way is from the nature of the efficient cause. In the world of sense we find there is an order of efficient causes. There is no case known (neither is it, indeed, possible) in which a thing is found to be the efficient cause of itself; for so it would be prior to itself, which is impossible. Now in efficient cause it is not possible to go on to infinity, because in all efficient causes following in order, the first is the cause of the intermediate cause, and the intermediate is the cause of the ultimate cause, whether the intermediate cause be several, or only one. Now to take away the cause is to take away the effect. Therefore, if there be no first cause among efficient causes

there will be no ultimate, nor any intermediate cause. But if in efficient cause it is possible to go on to infinity, there will be no first
efficient cause, neither will there be an ultimate effect, nor any intermediate efficient causes; all of which is plainly false. Therefore it
is necessary to admit a first efficient cause, to which everyone gives
the name of God."

The second way seems very similar to the first. The difference
however is in starting points, or the fact, or "effect", from which the
proof proceeds. As noted in regard to the first way this effect is
"motion"; in the second way it is "efficient causality". However, we
should carefully note that the effect is not efficient causality as such
but "an order of efficient causes". This means that we are really
dealing with are certain causes as effects of a prior cause. If the principle appealed to in the first way is: "whatever is in motion is moved
by another"; that in the second way may be put as: "whatever is an
ordinated efficient cause is caused to cause by another". The fact
that what is efficiently caused is an effect is self-evident. It is also self
evident that nothing causes itself in the same respect. Cause and effect go together, but one is named cause precisely because it is prior,
an agent, and the other is named effect precisely because it flows
from or after the cause, an effect.

Just as there is, strictly speaking, no self-mover, so there can be
no self-cause. A note on language use is required here also. Plato
used the word self-cause, as St. Thomas notes, but he meant the
same as uncaused, or what Aristotle meant by first cause. A cause is
defined as that which has influence unto the existence of another
dependent in existence. Looseness of expression, such as "everything must have a cause", can prompt those who do not pay atten-

tion to the evident intent of what is said to ask foolish questions like: "Who made God"?

Some are misled because of the real exercise of causality, such as most evidently belongs to the living, or to certain powers, such as free will. But what the objections made come from is not that the causal nature of vital "self movement", or of the free exercise of will power, does not exist, but that its ultimate dependence on an external cause is not easily seen or understood. The causality at these higher levels of being, however, do need to be understood in such a way that it does not eliminate the internal vitality of the animal or the true freedom of the will. God not only creates effects but also make some of them causes in their own right. The point is not to question the real causality belonging to such things but to recognise that, as created, it is of a secondary nature.

This misreading of the problem is indeed involved in the objection made by St. Thomas against himself in the very place in the *Summa Theologiae* where he deals with the proofs for the existence of God (*I, q. 2, art. 3 obj. 2*). The objection (in Latin and in English) is as follows:

Praeterea, quod potest compleri per pauciora principia, non fit per plura. Sed videtur quod omnia quae apparent in mundo, possunt compleri per alia principia, supposito quod Deus non sit, quia ea quae sunt naturalia, reducuntur in principium quod est natura; ea vero quae sunt a proposito, reducuntur in principium quod est ratio humana vel voluntas. Nulla igitur necessitas est ponere Deum esse.

"Further, it is superfluous to suppose that what can be accounted for by a few principles has been produced by many. But it seems that everything we see in the world can be accounted for by other principles, supposing God did not exist. For all natural things can be reduced to one principle which is nature; and all voluntary things can be reduced to one principle, which is human reason, or will. Therefore there is no need to suppose God's existence."

St. Thomas answers it as follows:

Ad secundum dicendum quod, cum natura propter determinatum finem operetur ex directione alicuius superioris agentis, necesse est ea quae a natura fiunt, etiam in Deum reducere, sicut in primam causam. Similiter etiam quae ex proposito fiunt, oportet reducere in aliquam altiorem causam, quae non sit ratio et voluntas humana, quia haec mutabilia sunt et defectibilia; oportet autem omnia mobilia et deficere possibilia reduci in aliquod primum principium immobile et per se necessarium, sicut ostensum est.

"Since nature works for a determinate end under the direction of a higher agent, whatever is done by nature must needs be traced back to God, as to its first cause. So also whatever is done voluntarily must also be traced back to some higher cause other than human reason or will, since these can change or fail; for all things that are changeable and capable of defect must be traced back to an immovable and self-necessary first principle, as was shown in the body of the Article."

The second part of the proof, as in the first way, leads us to the conclusion that in an ordered series of causes, where one cause is dependent for its causality upon another cause, there must needs be a first cause which itself is uncaused. That is to say, for the ultimate effect (which is not a cause) to occur there has to be a first independent cause (which is not an effect). For the intermediate causes only transmit what is originally supplied by the first cause to the last effect.

The same difficulty some have with accepting this proof applies as in the first way. For, the original cause is called first, not as if it were the first within the series of intermediate causes, but as a cause of quite opposite character to those in the series. It is to be taken, as it were, outside the series. This is not fully appreciated by those who think of a series in modern mathematical or numerical terms. For the first (and last) of a series of numbers are of exactly the same intent, just numbers occurring one after another or one before another. And so they tend to think of the series in question here in the same terms, indeed, as all to be counted within the one same series of intermediate effects/causes.

But the series of intermediate causes, which are also effects, differ in nature or character from the first cause, in that it is not an effect, and from the last effect, in that it is not a cause. The force of this part of the proof, therefore, lies in the fact that to explain what occurs one may very well do without the entire series of intermediate causes/effects (infinite or not) and have simply the (first) cause and the (last) effect. But, it would make no sense to do without the first cause and the last effect – for, as correlatives, a cause cannot be had without an effect, or an effect without a cause. Positing an infinity of intermediate causes/effects does not touch the issue of the dependence of something, which is a real last effect, upon something which is a real first cause.

This has some relevance to the way the proof needs to be understood and presented in the context of modern science. For a long series of intermediate causes is not as much a part of the notion of

natural causality in modern times as it was in ancient and mediaeval. In the course of nature we quickly come to an apparent first
cause. But this is of no great consequence to the conclusiveness of
the proof. It is only necessary to see natural causes as secondary or
intermediate causes. Such are not able to be held to be first causes,
for we are seeking a cause that is in no way an effect. But a natural
cause is as much an effect as any other created thing. Whether the
causes of which we know are traceable back a long way or short, or
infinitely, on the supposition considered by St. Thomas, does not
affect the argument. What is in no way an effect has to be what we
conceive as God. For in absolute terms of potency and act, and potency being conceived as receptive of something other than what it
actually is, it is pure act.

In the order of human affairs we are finally satisfied we have
reached the ultimate or first cause of an effect of human action
when we trace it back to an act of human will. Thus, in the example
generally used, we have a stone moved by a stick, by the hand, by
the members of the body, by the nervous system and so on, but finally by the will of the person involved. Why did the stone move?
Because so and so moved it which means because he willed to do so.
But this metaphysical principle of dependence applies as much to
spiritual created causes as to natural or physical or material causes.
In fact the human free will, though apparently acting from itself
alone, is necessarily subject to the divine will (as Lucifer found).

Today, however, if asked why the water became hot, we are satisfied with some natural cause (fire) or naturally induced cause, elec-
tricity, and do not ask to explain further. The series of intermediate
causes posited by the ancient cosmology is now seen as rather

quaint, the argument over infinite regress as an antiquated medievalism, a relic of a discredited natural science.

How do we establish that such natural causes, and even the spiritual action of the human will, must be accounted secondary, necessarily dependent upon a cause first in every respect? We simply need to demonstrate that they are intermediate causes, effect/causes, not first causes, but dependent for their causality upon an absolutely independent cause, about which we do not need to ask "Who or what caused it"? If we ask: "Why does God exist?" we may reply that he exists because of himself, but that is just a roundabout way of saying he is uncaused.

St. Thomas answers the question posed with the utmost economy, almost too briefly: causes in nature are evidently dependent causes; they cannot qualify as first causes; the human will is a deficient cause, it can fail and often does to achieve its object. So it cannot qualify as a first cause. A first cause itself uncaused is necessary ultimately to explain the existence of the effect. Though for ordinary natural explanations we can be satisfied with some natural cause; and for ordinary explanations of human productions we can be satisfied with discovering the person or will responsible, for ultimate intellectual or metaphysical satisfaction we cannot rest there. If it is a natural effect we need to go beyond a physical or natural cause; if it is an effect of human action we need to go beyond a human will.

All that remains then is to show that an absolutely first cause, or a cause in no way itself caused (or an effect) is something "to which everyone gives the name of God". To appreciate this we have to understand that we are reasoning in metaphysical terms, with words that are to be taken in all their universality. The existence of any effect demands the existence of a first cause of that effect. But this first cause cannot be in any way an effect. It is not sufficient to say that the independent source of the effect is so only in a certain order of causality. For that would make it not absolutely independent or un-caused; that is to say it would make it dependent on something else and thus an effect of some other cause. In common sense terms it would mean that the first cause would not be purely a cause, a crea-tor, but in some respect an effect, a creature. What is not a creature, however, is the very notion of God.

Let us, however, look at some of the more modern objections to this analysis of causality. Some are based upon the different concep-tion of (the range of) science, materially taken as "factual" or "em-pirical" knowledge. For some, the mere difference between modern and ancient science on this score automatically discredits the proof. This, however, as we have seen, involves a failure to address the real burden of the proof.

This is a difference between modern and Aristotelian thought based on the very concept of cause. For Aristotle it meant: "that which has influence unto the existence of some other thing depend-ent in existence" (and he listed not just the efficient cause but three other modes of cause). From this it can be seen that the concept of cause is not limited to material existence. Existence is a notion that is as wide as being. That is to say it has metaphysical import. There is no reason to limit its application to a cause within the physical world. Indeed, so far as the proofs for the existence of God are con-cerned it is obvious that they make no sense if the notion of cause is so narrowly interpreted.

But, as is well known, the modern era of philosophy and science is marked by a disdain for metaphysics. The roots of this go back to the late Middle Ages. It has necessarily affected the understanding of science, placed restrictions on the range of our reason, and consequently affected seriously our notions of logic and causality. The course of this bias leading to the total rejection of metaphysics as an intellectual discipline is something that we could trace in the history of modern philosophy from Francis Bacon and Rene Descartes.

But here we prefer to look more directly at how the new concept of cause was shaped by the success of Newtonian science. This confirmed the turn of the modern mind away from Metaphysics simply by focusing attention on science as now practically equated with Mathematics and Natural Science, not so much as independent sciences in their own right (as they were mainly in pre-modern thinking) but in what proved to be their most fruitful combination, the paradigm for which is modern physico-mathematics.

The subsequent interpretations of science, based upon the model of Newtonian science, were then fashioned mainly by the combined efforts of Hume and Kant. There were two sides to Newton's understanding of Natural Science, still then called Natural Philosophy, which appears from the name of his fundamental work: "Mathematical Principles of Natural Philosophy" ("Principia Mathematica Philosophiae Naturalis"). These two sides are the mathematical and the experimental.

Newton's genius was to develop a physico-mathematical science of enormous range that seemed to account for all the basic laws of "Physics". Mathematics had already come to dominate the minds of the new physical scientists, as in Descartes and Galileo. But Newton most successfully combined this powerful instrument of the mind with the English penchant for experimental science. Thus, his famous saying: *Non fingo hypotheses*, by which he meant his scientific laws and theories were solidly based in experience and experiment, unlike the "metaphysical" speculations of others, such, perhaps, as his rival, the great mathematician and German philosopher Leibniz).

But it is important to understand what this development in science meant with regard to what science had meant before. Aristotle, followed by St. Thomas, had already provided for this kind of physico-mathematical science in his division of the sciences. He called them medial sciences, partly natural, partly mathematical. Indeed, he clearly delineated Astronomy as such a medial science, neither purely a natural science nor purely a mathematical science.

The combination, however, was not merely incidental; in Aristotelian terms St. Thomas described a medial science as formally mathematical and materially natural. Nonetheless, the medial science is "substantially" physical; which means that the mathematics is subordinated to the natural science, or to the observational or experimental side of the science. Newton's achievement was the full flowering, as it were, of this combined scientific method, for he extended Mathematics so that it virtually took over the whole range of physical phenomena.

But, it is also to be carefully noted that alongside this development of Mathematics in modern times there was also a great surge in the experimental side of science. This was already becoming evident at the time of St. Thomas in his teacher St. Albert the Great, named the Universal Doctor among other things for his extraordinary contributions to the development of the experimental sciences. This was just as much due to the rediscovery of Aristotle's works on natural science, of his philosophy of nature, as on the other parts, such as Metaphysics and Ethics.

Albert embarked enthusiastically on the empirical study of nature precisely by reason of his recovery of the empirical spirit of Aristotle, unfortunately overlooked by most others, who simply took his scientific works "on authority". It was in the English scholastic world, however, such as in the Franciscan Roger Bacon, that the experimental spirit really took off. The experimental method inspired Francis Bacon, who became the official philosopher of empirical science as Descartes was coming to be regarded as the founder of the new mathematical philosophy.

As the new empirical science developed, however, it acquired an anti-Aristotelian bias. There were two reasons for this. Firstly, and nothing to do with Aristotle, and even against his explicit warnings, was the general tendency upon the discovery of the genius of the ancient Greek philosophy to take it on authority. This was against the spirit of Aristotle's thought, and most especially in the field of natural science. St. Albert and St. Thomas discerned this most clearly, but many others simply took on the whole corpus of ancient natural science as it was received.

The second reason, which was and is an almost inevitable fault with science, especially in its early development, was the tendency to speculate beyond what could be known by experience or experiment. This was, as has been noted, a human failing that Newton was keen to avoid. But even his genius was not immune to it, as is shown by the more recent developments of science. We would be foolish to imagine that today's science is free of it.

Aristotle himself took on much of the Greek natural science of his time and there was a great deal of speculative reasoning in his own thinking. Much of this proved to be erroneous on further more powerful observations and experimentation. This tended to discredit the whole scientific effort in the eyes of the new experimental scientists. Unfortunately, as is usually the case, the reaction went to the other extreme. The baby, as Americans put it, was thrown out along with the bathwater. What is intended here is that the notion of cause, which Aristotle had masterfully drawn in regard to the study of nature, was discarded and a truncated; part only of it was retained.

The "speculative" or rationalistic fault was thought to be connected with the notions of formal and final causality. So it was that the new concept of cause allowed for only the material cause and a notion of efficient cause that was interpreted materially, reducing it to the positing of pre-conditions associated with any effect or event. So the modern notion of cause in relation to the investigation of physical nature came to be virtually equated with pre-existing material elements or conditions.

The new notion of science, therefore, vindicated by the success of Newton, came to be seen in terms of physico-mathematics, with the mathematics providing the formal part and the new notion of empirical science providing the material part. Mathematics took over the position of queen of the sciences that had formerly been accorded to Metaphysics.

This was to have a profound effect upon the understanding of the capacity of human reason and the conception of the very processes of reasoning or logic. Hume was to take apart the notion of scientific necessity in regard to empirical science and induction, and Kant was to attempt to restore it by appealing to the accepted certainties in Newtonian science. This he did, though, by imposing, in a highly ingenious but artificial way, the *a priori* formal character of mathematics upon the inductive character of empirical science.

For Aristotle the movements of reason, or reasoning, mirror the complexity of the human intellectual make-up. Our knowledge has two origins, not one, namely, intellect and sense; it accordingly is a complex of universal and particular knowledge ("particular" being taken here in the sense of pertaining to an individual). Universal knowledge is proper to the intellect, but particular knowledge is common to intellect and sense, with sense having priority in this regard. We first sense the singular, then we understand by intellect alone the universal; then we understand the singular by the intellect working with the senses.

In regard to reasoning, or logic, then, we have a two-way movement; from particulars to universal and from universal to particulars. The former is called induction, the second deduction. But we need to be careful here not to confuse these rational processes in dealing with the division of the mind's acts into simple apprehension (the order of concepts), judgment (the order of propositions) and reasoning proper (the order of proof). For these two kinds of movements are reflected in the first two (apprehension and judgment) as well as the third (reasoning).

Furthermore, logical definitions are primarily of two kinds, ascending and descending. Universal propositions contained in principles (every triangle is a plane figure) may similarly be applied to particular propositions (this triangle is a plane figure). And, finally, reasoning may be inductive or deductive.

But there is a complication, or rather a refinement, which has generally been overlooked in the logic of the new scientific method. Deduction itself may proceed according to both directions; from cause to effect, which Aristotle called *a priori*, and from effect to cause (*a posteriori*). Reasoning in natural science, in which the intellect is most dependent upon the senses, is greatly dependent upon induction but not exclusively so. For sense data are particular effects to the intellect, from which it is possible to reason *a posteriori* to (universal) causes with logical necessity, or deductively, appropriate to physical science. Moreover, one is not limited to reasoning to causes that are within the natural order, or within natural science, so that such reasoning can prove at least the existence of supraphysical reality (of the spirituality of the human intellect and the existence of God).

According to the modern scientific mentality, however, there can only be quasi-mathematical judgments, with which after Kant the term *a priori* has been associated, and empirical experience, which is equated generally with induction, but with which after Kant the term *a posteriori* has tended to be associated. Hume emptied the notion of logical necessity of any rational value, so that *propter hoc* means no more than *post hoc*. At the same time he believed that he had demonstrated the basic logical ineffectiveness of scientific induction – thereby returning Newtonian science to *fingo hypotheses*.

Reducing the operation of the intellect to that of sense, he denied the ability of the intellect to draw out universals from particulars.

To Kant, the mathematical physicist, *cum* philosopher, inspired by the universality and necessity of Newton's laws of science, this was an intolerable conclusion. Yet he could not see any way out given the prevailing empiricist concept of our knowledge of the natural world, which had been partly promoted by Newton's insistence on strict adherence to the limits of experience and then had been brought to radical scepticism by Hume. After Hume's destructive criticism of the certainties alleged in the experiential approach to natural science, it was impossible to conceive that anything universal or necessary could come out of particulars, no matter how much co-incidence there appeared to be in nature. One could not observe the causal impulse passing from one billiard ball to another. Therefore one could only "reason" that the movement of one came after (*post*) that of the other, not on account of it (*propter*).All games were games of chance, and so too fundamentally was science.

Out of extreme intellectual frustration, Kant stood on his head, as it were, and took a fresh look at things. The universal was not obtained from the particulars; inspired by Copernicus Kant felt that one needed to reverse the positions of the two. Kant transferred the terms *a priori* and *a posteriori* to the order of judgment and pictured the process in terms of applying a universal and necessary proposition (*a priori* forms) to particular and contingent ones (empirical experience), like an artist "realising" his abstract idea or ideal form of a sculpture in a particular concrete work of art. He then set to work to "deduce" the logical order of necessary propositions, or *a priori* forms, required to give a philosophical defence of Newtonian physics. Such was the mentally artistic ability Kant was able to apply to the problem of scientific knowledge that he has fooled generations of "philosophers of science".

Philosophically it remained a compromise, and the subsequent history of modern philosophy is quite an involved story of attempts to hold together the tension between the logico-mathematical element belonging to Kant's contribution and the empiricist element derived from Hume's continuing influence. Dialectical Idealism was an immediate offspring of the former and Positivism of the latter. The deficiencies and contradictions of these solutions soon became evident and they have been followed by all sorts of ingenious attempts at refining Hume, as in Logical Positivism, and correcting the subjective formalism inherent in Kant and his Idealist followers, as in Existentialism.

But we cannot here go into these more general philosophical aspects of the legacy of Hume and Kant. We are primarily concerned to see how the concept of causality has been so changed in the process as to strip it (and science) of any objective necessity. On the one hand, formal causality became tied to mathematical forms, which abstract from any physical necessity, and on the other hand, physical phenomena came to be interpreted in merely materialistic terms so as to evacuate natural causality of any kind of necessity (not to be simply identified with logical necessity). Logic and mathematics became closely tied, and deduction became too exclusively *a priori*. *A posteriori* became confused with induction, and emptied of any intellectual value.

The only valid proofs of the existence of God are, as we have seen, *a posteriori* deductions from effect to cause. St. Thomas had noted that this kind of reasoning, when one passed outside the order of nature, could only establish the existence of things, not their proper nature. We have seen that there is no way of our knowing the nature or essence of God, which excludes an *a priori* proof. But we have sufficient rational means to prove the existence of God as the ultimate or first cause of the effects under consideration.

The appreciation of the proof from efficient causality therefore depends upon a proper understanding of nature and cause, which as we have seen is sadly lacking in modern science and thought generally. We have given some considerable attention to how this is so. So far as the notion of science is concerned, it comes down to narrowing science's range to the world of the objects of physical and mathematical science, and then focused on that kind of science that is a special combination of physics and mathematics. This peculiar combination of science St. Thomas well knew as medial. Furthermore, he is perhaps the only one who understood how to define it in Aristotelian terms.

It is one kind of science only because, in order for things to be one essentially the combination must be of a formal part and a material part; two forms essentially make two things. Thus he explained that the form was mathematical and the matter was physical. That is why Astronomy is a distinct science from Mathematics and Natural Science. Modern Physics is modelled on Astronomy.

The material/physical side and the formal/mathematical side both need to be proportioned to each other with the result that the mathematics is not pure mathematics and the physics is not pure physics. In relation to the physics of the science what this means is that mathematical form takes the place of natural forms (and ends).

This is congenial to the modern mind for besides having rejected Metaphysics it has also dismissed the notions of formal and final causality.

Though this distortion of the concept even of physical nature need not essentially affect the proof from efficient causality, it necessarily eliminates any recourse to the fourth and fifth ways. We will come back to this distortion in the modern mind's concept of nature and causality when dealing with these two proofs. Nonetheless, it also affects the capacity of the modern mind to follow the second way. For, the concept of nature had is basically materialist, and any one holding to a position of materialism is automatically atheist.

We have seen how the analysis of motion, which is excluded from pure mathematics, when applied to it in physico-mathematics, results in a peculiar treatment of the body in motion as inert (as if the same as at rest). In theory the body in motion is subject to the "principle" of inertia. That means we treat it as inert. But why does Newton not treat it as inert after subjected to a separate one off force that increases its speed or direction? Newton in fact is unconsciously applying the same principle of motion selectively because of his focus on mathematical analysis of the observed facts.

That is not an illegitimate selective process provided one does not pretend that the principle of inertia is of primary physical or natural import. It does not "wreck" St. Thomas's reliance on the metaphysical division of created reality into act and potency nor the metaphysical import of the principle of movement. Nevertheless, it underlies the difficulty some have, such as Hume had, with seeing how the cause of motion of a mobile body (second billiard ball) that has lost contact with the moving body (first billiard ball) can continue to be under the causal influence of the latter.

Such modern minds, especially if they have played billiards, when questioned, do not really deny that the first ball is quite evidently the cause of the motion of the second ball, regarding a denial as not only an insult to their intelligence but also to their playing ability. For it is their chosen use of the billiard cue that determines the motion and direction of the first billiard ball as a prior cause.

But, well "educated" in modern "physics", and fortified in the belief that what cannot be observed sensibly cannot be regarded as real, their native intellectual insight (had by a child before being compulsorily educated/indoctrinated in modern science) fails them. They are persuaded that the criticism of Anthony Kenny and other "Thomists" with a good knowledge of Newton's first law of motion, or should we not say lack of motion (inertia), "wrecks" St. Thomas's position on what accounts for the projectile in motion. "None so blind as those who will not (to) see" as the saying goes.

Despite the contrived difficulty (imagined rather than real) of seeing how the intervening influences are really connected as mover and moved; no one in fact is in any real doubt (real or imagined) about the causality involved. Nor should one be with regard to the principle of motion brought to bear: that whatever is in motion is so not from itself but from an extrinsic mover. I do not say external mover because the principle may be in the body being moved but as to what is undergoing the motion within the body. This principle is self-evident and of itself irrefutable. The modern principle of inertia only works to distract us from reflecting on the metaphysical principle.

Chapter 3

Existence of God – The Third Way

Tertia via est sumpta ex possibili et necessario, quae talis est. In-venimus enim in rebus quaedam quae sunt possibilia esse et non esse, cum quaedam inveniantur generari et corrumpi, et per consequens possibilia esse et non esse. Impossibile est autem omnia quae sunt, talia esse, quia quod possibile est non esse, quandoque non est. Si igi-tur omnia sunt possibilia non esse, aliquando nihil fuit in rebus. Sed si hoc est verum, etiam nunc nihil esset, quia quod non est, non inci-pit esse nisi per aliquid quod est; si igitur nihil fuit ens, impossibile fuit quod aliquid inciperet esse, et sic modo nihil esset, quod patet esse falsum. Non ergo omnia entia sunt possibilia, sed oportet aliquid esse necessarium in rebus. Omne autem necessarium vel habet causam suae necessitatis aliunde, vel non habet. Non est autem possibile quod procedatur in infinitum in necessariis quae habent causam suae ne-cessitatis, sicut nec in causis efficientibus, ut probatum est. Ergo necesse est ponere aliquid quod sit per se necessarium, non habens causam necessitatis aliunde, sed quod est causa necessitatis aliis, quod omnes dicunt Deum.

"The third way is taken from possibility and necessity, and runs thus. We find in nature things that are possible to be and not to be, since they are found to be generated, and to corrupt, and conse-quently, they are possible to be and not to be. But it is impossible for these always to exist, for that which is possible not to be at some time is not. Therefore, if everything is possible not to be, then at one time there could have been nothing in existence. Now if this were true, even now there would be nothing in existence, because that which does not exist only begins to exist by something already existing. Therefore, if at one time nothing was in existence, it would have been impossible for anything to have begun to exist; and thus even now nothing would be in existence—which is absurd. Therefore, not all beings are merely possible, but there must exist something the existence of which is necessary. But every necessary thing either has its necessity caused by another, or not. Now it is impossible to go on to infinity in necessary things which have their necessity caused by another, as has been already proved in regard to efficient causes. Therefore we cannot but postulate the existence of some being having of itself its own necessity, and not receiving it from another, but rather causing in others their necessity. This all men speak of as God."

The first thing to be noted about this third proof is the fact that it proceeds from an effect, as do all the five ways. In the first way the effect was motion itself, as it is found in bodies, in the second way the nature of a caused cause, which is found in physical things. In this third way it is what is called contingency in things, but as it is found initially in bodies. For all the proofs start from what is known through sense experience, in that it is from sense that the human intellect has to abstract the objects of its knowledge which issue in first concepts and propositions.

What is contingency so understood? It is the condition of a thing that exists obviously but can lose its existence. This is plain to see in all that is around us though in elementary things it may be hard to discern just as with minute change generally. A nanosecond is a period of time. With experience we come to realize that what characterizes physical or bodily existence is incessant change. It is so much so that the great Heraclitus claimed there are no things; there is just change. There is no water in the river but just pure "flow". That is nonsense even seen to be so by a child. But adults can come to take it seriously. It is the same with the modern idea of pure evolution.

However, the important thing to see in regard to this proof is that we do not have to hold that everything or every body in our experience is contingent. We can base the argument on the fact that some thing or body is contingent. For, we are not arguing from collectives but from natures, which are distributive in significance. We can prove for instance that every animal is mortal from the fact that it is a body made up of two or more parts. This fact we can gather from one animal that dies. If it corrupts or decomposes its nature must be composite. And what is composite can fall apart, can die, no matter how long it may actually live, or even if it is kept alive by something else forever. It has within the potential to die which is what being mortal means. Thus we will note that St. Thomas uses the fact that a contingent being is a thing that is possible not to be. Contingency belongs to things that are composite in some way, most fundamentally entitatively, in beings *(entia)* that are at least composed of *essentia* and *esse*.

But we are beginning with bodily things. Their existence *(esse)* is obviously not part of their essences. But they are doubly composite for their essences are composed of two essential parts, called by Aristotle substantial form and primary matter. It is this more complex composition that tricks up the modern critical interpreters of the third way. For when St. Thomas says that what is only possible to be can be not, this has to be applied first to bodily being where one thing in losing its form does not go totally out of existence but reduces into the primary matter out of which it came (necessarily drawn out by an extrinsic cause).

This deceives some into thinking that St. Thomas in speaking in terms of existence and non-existence in seemingly absolute terms has misstated what is happening. Primary matter has a certain permanence about it in that it is being as (pure) potency and is not non-being as Parmenides thought or even privation as Plato thought. But St. Thomas is speaking relatively here of generation and corruption in natural things after the fashion of Aristotle who discussed these changes originally in terms of being and non being. It is to be remembered that Aristotle was inventing the terms he had to use in order to express his insights into reality. The necessary clarification comes only as he proceeds to discuss these questions. So where bodies are concerned we have to first note existence and non existence as occurs relatively speaking when a body loses its substantial form and the primary matter takes on another. The first form has therefore ceased to be actually, but not potentially.

The next step in the proof extends the argument beyond the essential order to the entitative or existential order where the non existence spoken of is total. In fact in this part St. Thomas shifts to using the second way. But he could have simply applied the notion of contingency to the potency to be of essence or form taken without matter (as he does elsewhere as we shall see).

Thus one may see that many moderns sunk in materialist thinking miss the fundamental point of the proof, thinking we have to be concerned with things as they are temporal and spatial, that is to say with only physical things. They are not capable of breathing in the rarefied air of Metaphysics. So it is that the two words they mix up from the very beginning are the very basic ones of existence and matter. Without a proper understanding of them one cannot even properly understand contingency.

Existence (*esse*) as understood by St. Thomas means nothing to them. On the other hand matter means everything. For not having a clue about what Aristotle means by primary matter they take it for what is understood as secondary matter, namely, matter that is under some form or other. For primary matter being pure potency cannot exist unless it is under some form. Such a notion of matter is like that of "stuff", bodily things taken most generally, which is then confused with the logical genus of material substance or just body, any body.

One may imagine the mental chaos that ensues from such a position. It is not so much a condition of ignorance as of incorrigible misunderstanding. Having taken the wrong turning at the first fork in the road all subsequent "progress" in science leads only further and further away from the due destination. Having erred in principle as Aristotle says one errs without hope of correction by any intellectual or rational means. One can only hope for a supernatural rescue.

When the argument from contingency is applied to the material order only what the modern mind sees is that the loss of existence by one material form of being does not mean total annihilation. For the matter remains (under another form) in which the form lost still exists potentially. Then inevitably the modern materialist conceives of matter as existing under some form, not the same form, but in a process of change of one form for another *ad infinitum,* and therefore we may posit matter as necessarily existing despite the fact that all forms may cease to exist – for we have surreptitiously conferred form and hence the act of existence on matter. This mistaken notion of matter was already in Suarez who was taken to be faithfully representing Aquinas.

We can imagine matter persisting under some other form ad infinitum. So the *quandoque* (at some time) St. Thomas uses is taken as occurring within time. It is not God that needs to be what explains the existence and non existence of all forms of being but just a general notion of matter. We use the word imagine advisedly. For though we cannot speak of pure potency as really existing by itself we can imagine it doing so just as we imagine time before time and place outside the physical universe.

That is reinforced by our need to express the non temporal and non spatial (angels and God) in terms of time and place, when and where. But it is only imaginary time and place (space). Indeed, even in the order of material being the relation between things and time and place has been reversed. In truth when and where are accidental features of material things or "matter". They are quantitative measures of bodily change. But deceived by the mathematical abstraction that puts quantity before all other accidents the modern mind makes these measures the fundamental container of all material substance. Everything therefore must be considered to be in time and space in order to exist. Kant then made these measures *a priori* forms of our very knowledge (sensibility) not just of our empirical experience but underlying (or overlaying) all human theoretical knowledge.

This further mixes up the logical use of "is" with the metaphysical use in regard to reality, as when we say nothing is or was (*fuit*). Even when we are speaking of the very opposite of nothing, what infinitely transcends the order of bodily things, motion, place and time, as with the notion of eternity, we are constrained to use such words as "was" with regard to the divine as is evident with our speaking of the persons of the Trinity. The Word of God was in the beginning, was with God the Father and so on.

So anyone affected (infected) in the least by the underlying materialism of modern scientific thinking, be he/she scientist, philosopher or theologian will be completely befuddled and talk nonsense. One may try to enter into a discussion of the proof with them but to no avail. For since they are stuck in a time warp they will always come back to the permanence of matter as "necessarily" underlying the contingency of individual things under some form or other that continually appears and disappears. The discussion has to be interminable and go around in circles coming back to the original mistaken notions it begins with.

So we have to root out this deep-seated malignity in our modern mentality. This is necessarily a difficult and delicate surgical operation involving much personal pain. We had rather not think about it. So it is that we have to extract the strictly temporal connotation attaching to such terms as "at some time", "when", "was" and so on that seem to be integral to the proof.

But before we do this it may be better to preface a treatment of contingency in regard to material reality by that which may be applied directly to created spiritual reality. Though we cannot apodictically prove the existence of separated substances such as angels we can know metaphysically what is a pure substantial form or essence free of matter. Indeed this is how St. Thomas presented the proof for the existence of God in one of the first of his metaphysical works *De ente et essentia*. A sign of the profound ignorance of all today in this regard is the fact that when I try to use this most famous title of St. Thomas the "spell-checker" (appropriately a mindless robot) constantly (no matter how many times I put the words together) changes *essentia* to "essential", the programmer clueless no doubt of even this word's philosophical meaning.

Such is the mountainous mudslide of mechanical thinking one is up against today in trying to defend the rationality of St. Thomas's proofs, even within the close circle of the current Catholic intelligentsia. However, let us soldier on. The simple proof depends upon recognizing that the essence of every creature does not provide a reason for positing that the being by which it is defined exists in reality. Of itself it only can be. Essence names potency to esse, its form is a "can be". It is the act of existence that is the act of be. Consequently, since what has an essence (potency to be), that is a being, as we know it (*ens*), does exist, we have to look outside its essence to explain this fact.

Being as we know it needs then to be understood as a composite concept, composed of two entitative parts, essence and esse. Because our intellect is focused on essences, forms or natures, we tend to forget we are dealing primarily with beings (*entia*, not mere *essentiae*) as they exist. Esse tends to fade into the background, to be just taken for granted, even though Aristotle said that we cannot really know what things or real substances are unless we first know that they are. When we realize that we have to look outside the whole essential order of substances, material and spiritual, to account for existence we find it only in the act of existence itself that attaches to every existing thing.

This applies not only in accounting for the existence of things but also for the existence of what they produce or reproduce. Everything tends to produce its like, living things reproduce their own kind. But what does that mean? They are not only things in their own right but they are also causes of the existence of other things.

But this natural causality is operative precisely at the level of form, nature or essence. Things have influence unto the existence of others but only according to them having the same form, in the order of essence; we can produce our like, as the dog produces beings with the form of dog. But the form of dog belongs to the essential order. It cannot account for the existence of any dog, absolutely speaking. In the end we have to account for the existence of everything by reference to some being that has the "form" or act of esse, not mere essence as potency for esse.

We may thank existing dogs for the coming into being of other dogs. But this cannot leave God out of account. Thank God for dogs. We love them just for what they are, indeed just for "being around". Created causes act under the superior causal influence of one who can give existence itself. That is because this one being is pure *esse*, the *actus purus* of St. Thomas. The owner of esse is the first cause; the receivers of esse, all natural or created things, are second causes, participators, to be sure, in the ineffable generosity of God, but not the first to be accounted responsible for the existence of their effects.

The existence of God comes so quasi-immediately to all minds and lips that even the most committed atheist utters the expression "Thank God", as it were before thinking, when he or she considers any and every thing that exists. On reflection, however, his fundamental "faith" in the materialism underpinning his education/training in "Science" suppresses this sentiment so that he turns in disdain from such an "unscientific" thought. Nonetheless, he continues to speak out loud this quasi-instinctive intellectual expression when, as Hume would put it, he exits his "philosophical club" and returns to the street on his way home.

It is St. Thomas who has brought out most brilliantly the fact that existence and God go together necessarily whereas all other beings only possess existence contingently. For it is not our ordinary notion of existence, which comes from *ex sistere,* Latin for "to stand outside" (one's causes) which is appropriate for all created effects that is applicable in the case of God. The dependency upon something else has to be taken from the notion when applied to God. That is now obvious, just as "caused" has to be evacuated from cause in the second way, and "moved" from "mover" in the first. So too will any notion of being made (*per-fectum*) according to an idea in some other intelligence have to be eliminated from most perfect in the fourth way and ordered from that of orderer in the fifth.

Motion is act but obviously most deficient of all as it flows from forms in primary matter, which is that level of being that is pure potency and nearest to nothing. Contingent beings are actual but still deficient in terms of existence because their essence names only a potency. The first and third proofs then more directly stem from our understanding of the basic division of (created) being into act and potency; the other three from the three kinds of effects that depend upon the three kinds of extrinsic causality (efficient, exemplary and final). All lead to the one being (*ens*) that is not composed of *essentia* and *esse*, that is not complex or manifold but *simplex* (*sine plex*, without fold), because consisting only of the supreme act of *esse*, pure act.

Thus the proof from contingency when applied to beings that have pure substantial form or simple essence (without matter) is clearly seen by one whose metaphysical insight has not been darkened by bad will or bad education. Sadly, that the state of intellectual blindness that is the general condition of mankind (and womankind) since the Fall; but it has been cured, thank God, since the coming of Christ and his institution of the Catholic Church. However, God does not act in human affairs except with and through the consent of human wills. This could not be otherwise but it is an effect of the divine goodness in giving such creatures the possibility of doing what they do out of a perfect love that is free.

Some therefore can choose to "go their own way", expressed by perhaps the most intelligent of the angels in his *non serviam*. This most foolish act of will, the sin of pride, has to be accompanied by the grossest of intellectual errors, and to have the most dire consequences. The angels can only make one choice in this regard. Luckily, human beings can "repent" (think again); and so the history of salvation even since the beginning of Christianity has been a battle again the "forces of evil", both angelic and in our own bad inclinations and choices. Freedom is a two edged sword.

These considerations do not belong directly to the proof but are put to explain the fierce opposition that has arisen against it even from "members of one's own household". It seems that the blindness of mind and hardness of heart of humanity returns with greater force in post-Christian countries than it was in pre-Christian. Chesterton observed that in regard to sexual depravity the sins of the so-called modern Christian world have far surpassed that of the ancient pagan. The same may be said, as he did, not only of the sins against the sixth commandment and the natural institution of marriage, but also of the sins against the seventh and the natural institution of property.

A short extract about sex from his essay on "Sex and Property" is given below. The essay deserves to be read in full today when things are even worse than they were in his day 100 years ago.

"In one way all this ancient sin was infinitely superior, immeasurably superior, to the modern sin. All those who write of it at least agree on one fact; that it was the cult of Fruitfulness. It was unfortunately too often interwoven, very closely, with the cult of the fruitfulness of the land. It was at least on the side of Nature. It was at least on the side of Life. It has been left to the last Christians, or rather to the first Christians fully committed to blaspheming and denying Christianity, to invent a new kind of worship of Sex, which is not even a worship of Life. It has been left to the very latest Modernists to proclaim an erotic religion which at once exalts lust and forbids fertility."

He sums up the immoral state of the modern world (that boasts of its "Western values"): "But even the stink of decaying heathenism has not been so bad as the stink of decaying Christianity. The corruption of the best…".

The sins against the fifth commandment are even more pronounced, the just past twentieth century being described by an American Jesuit whose cause for canonization has begun, the Venerable Fr. John Hardon (1914-2000), as the most homicidal in all human history. That might be said if the explosion in our times in the number of abortions of the most innocent of human beings in the wombs of their mothers were not counted.

With regard to the eighth commandment the stench of deceit that issues from the communications media may be gathered from a statement repeated publicly by Fr. Hardon quoting Marshall McLuhan: "The modern media is engaged in a Luciferan conspiracy against the truth".

We leave the readers to draw their own conclusions with regard to the first four commandments. That, then, is the "moral" context in which the proofs for the existence of God have to be received. Is it any wonder that many an argument is put against proof of the existence of God? Is it any coincidence that this is presaged by "scientific" denial of the existence of the devil and the exaltation of human freedom from the moral law? For a more extensive treatment of these matters I refer the readers and students to my book "Ethics Today and Saint Thomas Aquinas".

But we return to the intellectual difficulties put up against the third way of St. Thomas that focus on his assertion that all contingent bodies necessarily together do not exist "at some time". We have seen the evident truth of this in respect of contingent spirits. For their existence has to come from outside their essences so they have "not to be" before they were given existence. The same conclusion follows that if such contingent being were all that is then there would have to have been "at some time" in the spiritual world absolute nothing.

The same applies obviously to composite essences but this is where matter comes into the picture and to the rescue of the atheist/materialist who wishes to argue that the situation is different. For, standing on one's head, one can imagine matter on top and existence on the bottom of the scale of reality. Then, imaginatively we can picture matter as the eternal reservoir of be-ing.

After all, Aristotle himself was prepared to concede that "matter", i.e. secondary matter, was "eternal". Yet, strangely enough, this did not prevent him from asserting the eternal existence of God. Clearly, we have two meanings of "eternal". Indeed, there are three, the contingent material, the contingent spiritual and the necessary divine. It is only the third, however that excludes such eternalness being "at some time" nothing. The other two readily accommodate not being, or nothingness, if existence is not given to them "when" God wills to. That contingent being be the only existing form of be-ing is self-contradictory. That is the basis of the third way, the proof from contingency.

The modern critics, helped by the materialism underlying modern science, fool themselves that matter, as the least level of being in material things, makes a difference. They simply cannot conceive the obvious fact that matter is the furthest removed from existence, that pure potency is the nearest to nothing. Matter, properly conceived as an essential part of a body, can only exist through form. And form itself as we have seen is but essence as potential only for existence.

Embroiled in the coils of time the modern mind cannot think metaphysically or rather explicitly rejects that level of human intellect. It cannot rise about the level of the physical bodily world. And it is not freed from this materialist cave by introducing the mode of thinking that is Mathematics. That only re-enforces, by means of quantic concepts that are rooted in matter, its notion of potential infinity, also derived from the deficiency of being pertaining to matter.

This deficiency in thinking flows on unfortunately into the minds of the modern Catholic interpreters of the five ways. Unconscious of the malign influence of their "compulsory, secular and free" education ("free" meaning paid for by the State, or rather the creditors, bond-holders, of the State who wish to conserve their privileged proprietary status), all are to some extent indebted to the State that "looks after them". But be careful if a whiff of this dependence gets out – you might in Orwell's language be declared an enemy of the State.

Regrettably, one has to put these comments in such strong terms. There seems no other way to bring fellow "intellectual" Catholics at least to their senses. It is no minor matter to defend the proofs for the existence of God in a time when religion and morals themselves are being "officially" ridiculed and more and more aggressively attacked. The third way has become, for the reasons indicated, a particular target.

Let us now move on to consider the fourth way.

Chapter 4

Existence of God – The Fourth Way

*Quarta via sumitur ex **gradibus** qui in rebus inveniuntur. Invenitur enim in rebus aliquid magis et minus bonum, et verum, et nobile, et sic de aliis huiusmodi. Sed magis et minus dicuntur de diversis secundum quod **appropinquant** diversimode ad aliquid quod maxime est, sicut magis calidum est, quod **magis appropinquat** maxime calido. Est igitur aliquid quod est**verissimum, et optimum, et nobilissimum**, et per consequens **maxime ens**, nam quae sunt **maxime vera**, sunt **maxime entia**, ut dicitur II Metaphys. Quod autem dicitur maxime tale in **aliquo genere, est causa omnium quae sunt illius generis,** sicut ignis, qui est maxime calidus, est causa omnium calidorum, **<u>ut in eodem libro dicitur</u>**. Ergo est aliquid quod omnibus entibus est causa esse, et bonitatis, et cuiuslibet perfectionis, et hoc dicimus Deum.*

"The fourth way is taken from the <u>gradation</u> to be found in things. <u>Among</u> beings there are some more and some less good, true, noble and the like. But 'more' and 'less' are predicated of different things, according as they <u>resemble</u> in their different ways something which is the maximum, as a thing is said to be hotter according as it <u>more nearly resembles</u> that which is hottest; so that there is something which is <u>truest, something best, something noblest</u> and, consequently, something which is <u>uttermost being</u>; for those things that are greatest <u>in truth</u> are <u>greatest in being</u>, as it is written in Metaph. ii. Now the <u>maximum in any genus is the cause</u>

of all in that genus; as fire, which is the maximum heat, is the cause of all hot things. Therefore there must also be something which is to all beings the cause of their being [to be], goodness, and every other perfection; and this we call God."

We ought first note what is here the effect in question. But here again we have to repeat a complaint about the English translation. Compared to the Latin it is a mess, as usual, and I have indicated the particular mistranslations by putting the corresponding words and phrases of the Latin in bold type and of English with underlining. In one case I have underlined the bold phrase in Latin to indicate it is simply left out in the English. The translator no doubt thought it was of no consequence but that is a good instance of a translator abandoning his task of translating faithfully what is in the original and inserting his own opinion about what is said. In this case it may not be of any great consequence but it may be useful to know that St. Thomas got the thought from Aristotle in the same place as he has earlier indicated.

The first bald failure to translate the word that is there in the text is the substitution of the abstract form for the concrete, of "gradation" for "grades". It is important especially in this context to preserve the sense of the real individual existence of the effects. Words such as "gradation" are like "humanity" compared to "neighbour". Love of "humanity" is fine in the abstract but it is not the same as loving one's neighbour, with all his or her existing individual attributes. The shock of the real takes an effort to adjust to. But as noted before it is a feature of English as used commonly and so the translator simply ignores the form of the word and (thereby thinking again that it is of no consequence) undercuts the existential force of the Latin. Then his English speaking readers wonder why the argument somehow falls flat.

How does "approaches" get translated as "resembles"? Do you resemble someone more the more you approach him? Of course there is a sense in which the word "approach" may be so taken. But why try to anticipate St. Thomas's argument?

One can see where the swap has come from. For, similarity does come into the argument. But the platonic notion of resemblance or remembrance is something that has to be avoided. Much of the discussion of the proof in terms of "participation" has this fault. The platonic notion works from ideas as cause to physical things as effect. To posit beings as participations of divine being is to proceed the same wrong way, which supposes the conclusion before the premises. All five proofs have to work from effect to cause. From the point of view of pure reason it is a mistake in elementary understanding of logic, more prevalent perhaps in those of Faith who are certain already of God's existence.

The core of the proof lies in the fact that we cannot make comparisons between things except by reference to a superlative. The relative necessarily supposes the absolute. But it is the creature/effect that approaches the creator/cause, not working both ways, as speaking initially in terms of resemblance might suggest.

In causal terms where we are dealing with things that are similar in any way and differ by degrees or otherwise we need to posit the existence of a thing that is the exemplar, the standard one thing, according to which they can be compared. This applies most obviously in comparing and measuring the quantity of things where a standard measure is needed. But there are important differences in the method of comparison at different levels of being, as will be shown below with regard to the different objects of our intellectual knowledge, in metaphysics, mathematics and physics.

We are most familiar with the principle that every comparative supposes a superlative in relation to measurement in terms of quantity. Aristotle famously defined measure as that by which a quantity is known. But here we may be misled into thinking that there is no greatest or smallest, for by mathematical abstraction we enter the area of the potentially infinite. The principle upon which the proof relies is least applicable in Mathematics, relatively applicable in Physics, and absolutely in Metaphysics, as we shall see. This is because of the influence of potency and matter on act and form, which latter is where the principle takes us to the actually infinite.

Quantity being the first property of bodies derived from primary matter manifests the deficient nature of potency compared to act. So the examples used by St. Thomas are not taken from numbers but from natural forms of physical reality. The objects of Mathematics abstract from sensible qualities and even from the action that is motion.

Thus, the mathematician does not think in terms of goodness, except in the least respect that it denotes something of beauty of quantitative form (as of shape and shapeliness). So it is that whilst in quantitative comparisons there is some idea of the greater there is no notion of the absolute best or even the greatest. It is important to note this because the modern mind even in the consideration of physical things is focused on the mathematical side of the medial science of physico-mathematics. This deeply affects its assessment of proofs that transcend the order of quantity. So even in regard to physical qualities and forms there is no sense of a best. For the measure that is applied is quantitative. St. Augustine notes that we use the language of quantity even in regard to spiritual forms and qualities. But he says when we say greater in this context we are to take the meaning in terms of goodness, i.e. as meaning better.

Though there is a unit whereby we measure quantities it is not a natural unity when applied to physical qualities. We have to adopt one (small) weight as a measure if we are to compare the weights of things. We cannot measure lengths of actual bodies unless we select one part length to use as the unit. That is the measure, the standard rod, or other sensible thing that is selected and kept from outside things such as heat that might affect it. Conceived and imagined in terms of a line, quantities are potentially divisible ad infinitum, with no absolute unitary beginning or end. The principle and term of a line are not parts of the line but simply mark its limit. Physically considered, quantity such as the surface of a body is but the limit of its qualitative accidents, such as colour and texture.

But even with physical qualities such as heat the modern mind thinks of measures quantitatively. Again the modern scientist is ignorant of the differences between qualities even as set out in Aristotle's Categories. Aristotle classifies them into four main kinds, habits and dispositions, powers and impotencies, sensible qualities and affections and shape and shapeliness. Then in regard to powers there is the most important distinction between active and passive powers.

This becomes important when we note that sensible qualities, such as the sensation of heat, are considered relative to sense powers (such as touch) whose goodness depends upon proportion and is obviously not to be taken in absolute physical terms. So we have to be careful in judging the greatness of heat to note the difference between it as a form of physical activity (motion) and a sensible quality. These and other distinctions complicate the use of comparison in physical reality. The main distinction is between act and potency at the level of form and matter. It is acts and forms that are primarily comparable in terms of being. It is these that will take us to the superlative act and being, the actually infinite God, not potency and what comes from primary matter, namely, quantity, which is "measured" only by the potentially infinite.

The distinctions needed when discussing these things in relation to our sense knowledge are particularly relevant because the passive nature of the powers of sense knowledge are strictly relative to these sensible qualities. What is the best kind of sight? We must take into account not only the individual but also the species. Is not the eagle's better than the owl's? Not from the viewpoint of the owl. In regard to human nature, it would be unsuitable to have either. For the senses of man (and woman) are adapted to a middle range so as to be perfectly suited to his higher intellectual and rational nature.

The application of the principle is relative in the differences in natures in the physical order of things. There the natural is the best, as Aristotle noted, but many material obstacles both internal and external prevent physical things from reaching their natural end or perfection, which in any case is but temporal and fleeting. We can assess what is better and best at this level, but it is more in terms of being between species rather than individuals within a species. A dog is a better being than a daffodil though we may be able to consider one daffodil better than another and even believe we have found the best. But this application of the principle of comparison is still only relative where actual forms of bodily things are concerned. For primary matter has a potentially infinite "appetite" for natural forms and so we cannot say that a better or more beautiful daffodil may not be found, if not in the present, in the future. That is the problem with using physical examples, not only as relative to our sense knowledge, but also considered intellectually as different forms of being.

This applies also to the example of fire used by St. Thomas, not as "the maximum heat", as the translator blithely states, but as fire was thought to be the hottest thing. The ancients could say so on the basis of their natural science. But even so this could only be according to knowledge of things as present actually within their experience. It does not prevent a hotter thing coming out of primary matter, as explained above. So there is no "best" or greatest hot body except in relative terms. This can be useful knowledge even from a scientific point of view. But it cannot have any absolute character.

This and other considerations are used in an effort to compromise St. Thomas's argument. But they are mis-conceived for the same reason that criticisms of his other proofs are. They are from people who cannot lift their minds above the lower material level of physical and mathematical being. It is no wonder that the modern mind, captured by the idea of "matter" and a materialist notion of "evolution", "measuring" everything in mathematical terms, cannot make any sense of St. Thomas's proofs. Thus, we have materialists such as Richard Dawkins offering criticism of this proof by asking what is the greatest in smells.

We should judge St. Thomas's use of the example of heat, in the physical thing that is fire, for what it is, an illustration. The virtue of an illustration lies in its illustrative quality, not its truth. He used it as an illustration in the context of the mistaken ancient physics of his time. That however does not affect the usefulness of the illustration. Indeed, on the assumptions of ancient physics it is more illustrative of the principle being relied upon.

Aristotle noted that natures are the measure of natural goodness and some natures are higher or better than others. Indeed we can know that human nature in the human person is the most perfect in all natures within the natural world. But that is because it transcends that order by having a spiritual soul. Otherwise, as said above, we can make comparisons based on actual or formal differences but as they are affected by matter. Thus within human experience, or updated empirical science, we may detect what can be judged (for the time being) the best whereby to compare the relative goodness or ontological worth of the rest.

That is enough to give us the idea of the principle of comparison that can then be most properly applied in the order of things and forms that transcend the material order of reality. These are the notion of being (*ens*) itself and its common modes called transcendental, such as the good, true, beautiful and even the one, which provides the ontological notion of an absolute measure. Also able to be the subject of metaphysical comparisons are spiritual qualities, such as intelligence and love. (The best level of being the modern mentality can come up with is that of carnal knowledge and sexual love, the former appropriated in the law as the name for a crime, and the latter for the legalization of an unnatural vice).

The fact, however, that we can say some things (*entia*) are better than others in such transcendental terms means that there must exist a thing that is the best thing *(ens)* absolutely. This best thing will then be the measure whereby all things that "resemble" one another in this regard are to be judged as better or worse, i.e. more good or less good (taken initially without any moral overtones). This best will necessarily be "without measure" or measureless, for it is that which measures not that which is measured. That is the conclusion the argument takes us to.

For reasons opposite to those applying where matter is involved we cannot know directly the nature of this exemplar of being itself. But we can know it indirectly through the very effects that demand its existence. Then when God reveals something of his (triune) nature we have a real knowledge upon which to base our assessment of all created beings especially in regard to their spiritual qualities.

When these considerations have been taken into account St. Thomas can readily take us to the logical conclusion, which is both formally valid and conclusive of the truth that what we call God exists.

It may be noticed that one needs to spend little time on the proof itself (as St. Thomas did) once we have cleared away the root causes of the obstacles and difficulties allegedly associated with it, mostly put up by supposed Catholic experts on the philosophy or theology of religion, those that is who are not simply dismissing the proofs as not worthy of serious consideration.

We will therefore finish with some supplementary comments upon the defects in translations and thinking related to the presentation of the proof in English. I pass over the mistranslation of *veris-*

simum, et optimum et noblissimum, the truest, best and noblest **thing**, all taken together in the one thing, by "something truest, something best, something noblest", taken as three separate things, and come to *maxime ens* as "uttermost being". What can that English expression mean when the same word "being" is used later to translate *esse?* Does the translator think that *ens* and *esse* are the same word in Latin or does he consider the difference is of no consequence? But he is not alone in translating these two Latin words with the vague English word "being". You would be hard put to find any translation where the two words are properly distinguished.

That mistake alone undermines the whole logic of the argument. We may then be persuaded of the fallacy of the fourth way as Norris Clarke was of the third, who is quoted as saying: "The third, from contingency, is formally invalid as it stands, based on a logically invalid principle, uncritically taken over from Aristotle ..." (quoted by Michael Augros in "Aquinas's Tertia Via", Angelicum, 2006). St. Thomas obviously does not know what he is talking about. Aren't we lucky to be living in the twenty first century?

There is a more subtle misleading translation even though the words can have the meaning on their face. That comes from a confusion of the logical order with the real in the use of the word genus. This is used in a real sense (which St. Thomas often uses elsewhere). In using the example of fire St. Thomas is obviously thinking of it according to the understanding of his times, as the hottest **thing** (in the genus of hot **things**).We know differently. But it does not affect the argument; for illustrations are not used to say something true but to illustrate.

So, having gained an idea of the truest, best and noblest in the order of beings (*entia*), we go looking for the thing in which they are realised. This leads us to the conclusion that they must all exist in the one being, in which *ens* is the same as *esse*. In terms of the logical connection between the imperfect and the perfect, that is the gist of the fourth way.

Michael Augros has used his own translation in his treatment of the fourth way. This is a much better translation than the ones regularly used and is one reason why his appreciation of the proof is much better than most of the circle of modern day critics against whom he feels compelled to defend the reputation of St. Thomas. For if one does not have an accurate translation of the terms used in the proof nor an understanding of the truth of the propositions in the premises it not likely that one will see the validity and truth of the conclusion. Given the superior estimation of most moderns of their own intelligence compared to that of St. Thomas it is not surprising that they attribute the deficiency they see in this and the other proofs to the weakness of mind of St. Thomas and Aristotle rather than to their own.

Of recent times there is a host of commentators who have come to "improve on" the presentation of St. Thomas, bringing in all sorts of related principles in aid, such as the platonic notion of participation mentioned. Another is the henological principle. This is named from the Greek *enas* for "one". The "h" comes from the proclitic that is added to the sound as in the pronunciation of the word for Greek itself. As the notion of participation goes back to Plato, this use of the notion of one goes back to Plotinus. If used to argue *a posteriori* from the existence of many possessing different "degrees" of being to the one supreme being it is but an application of the fourth way to the transcendental one, rather than the good. But if it seeks to take the argument in the same way the Platonist takes it, arguing from the idea of the one to explain the existence of the many, as from the whole to the participators, then it suffers from the same *a priori* fault. It tries to explain the existence of the effects from the supposed cause, knowledge of which is assumed to be had either as by Plato with his ideas, or by the Christian with his Faith.

This platonic fault was picked up by Aristotle and recognised by St. Thomas. A common mistake is to fail to distinguish transcendental one from predicamental one. The former applies to all being, the latter as well to bodies because it is from the order of quantity. Aristotle had already noted the error in Plato, probably had from the influence of Mathematics in his philosophy. Of course in modern times the confusion is all but universal.

So the secular modern mind would not be impressed with this version of the proof. But the modern religious mind, seeking to overcome the evident "deficiencies" in St. Thomas's fourth way, with him relying on principles "uncritically taken over from Aristotle", goes to the extent of asserting that St. Thomas was as much a Platonist, despite his adoption of Aristotle's stern criticism of Plato precisely in this regard.

We could go into the other features of Plato's philosophy which stem from him preferring the evidence of the internal sense of the imagination to the evidence of the external senses, so that he and his strict followers are inevitably "out of touch" with the real world and live in the world of their own ideas. That subjectivism has been revived with a vengeance in the modern age, with Descartes and Kant, most powerfully assisted by the triumph of Newton's mathematical physics whose dominant influence continues despite relativist and "quantum" adjustments because of observational aberrations to the absolutist and determinist character of his laws.

St. Augustine avoided the errors of Plato by putting the ideas as prototypes of natures in the mind of God. But that is of no rational help in proving God's existence in the first place. St. Thomas interpreted this great mind so as to avoid it being used in support of philosophical Idealism. But many others are not so free from such a subtle error. They would do well to pay greater attention and more respect to the proofs, based on a sound metaphysics, to be found in Aristotle and St. Thomas.

It is to be remembered that, where created effects are concerned, God is the supreme artist, and the way to his mind, as with any great artist, is through his works of art. Do we have any doubt of Beethoven's musical genius? Is it because we have personal experience of his existence? Do we doubt that the author of these sublime works, regardless of the name by which he went, must have existed? His effects belong to only one category of being, and that in the accidental order of sound. All the more can we be sure of the eternal existence of God, from his present effects that span the whole of reality, of substance and of accident.

St. Thomas's fourth way focuses on the transcendental good. This brings in the first of the two objections generally put prior to consideration of all five ways. It has particular application to this aspect of the fourth. For the objection raises the deep and disturbing prevalence of evil in human affair, present throughout all history since the Fall, but seemingly reaching a crescendo type climax in our own times.

The two journalist brothers, Christopher and Peter Hitchins, have both been in the thick of things in a century described as the most homicidal in all human history. They both have spent a large part of their working life in the "hottest" spots on the globe, Peter particularly in Communist Russia and Christopher (now deceased) in the Middle East. The latter so reacted to the evil that he lost faith in a good (great) God. On the other hand, the former gave up his atheism and became a champion of Christianity.

The existence of evil is not a valid objection against the evidence for the existence of a good God, as St. Thomas had already shown. For the only rational explanation of the presence of such evil is that it is from the bad use of free will, the inhumanity of man towards his fellow man.

Let us move on then to consider the fifth way.

Chapter 5

Existence of God – The Fifth Way

Quinta via sumitur ex gubernatione rerum. Videmus enim quod aliqua quae cognitione carent, scilicet corpora naturalia, operantur propter finem, quod apparet ex hoc quod semper aut frequentius eodem modo operantur, ut consequantur id quod est optimum; unde patet quod non a casu, sed ex intentione perveniunt ad finem. Ea autem quae non habent cognitionem, non tendunt in finem nisi directa ab aliquo cognoscente et intelligente, sicut sagitta a sagittante. Ergo est aliquid intelligens, a quo omnes res naturales ordinantur ad finem, et hoc dicimus Deum.

"The fifth way is taken from the governance of the world. We see that things which lack intelligence, such as natural bodies, act for an end, and this is evident from their acting always, or nearly always, in the same way, so as to obtain the best result. Hence it is plain that not fortuitously, but designedly, do they achieve their end. Now whatever lacks intelligence cannot move towards an end, unless it be directed by some being endowed with knowledge and intelligence; as the arrow is shot to its mark by the archer. Therefore some intelligent being exists by whom all natural things are directed to their end; and this being we call God."

There are a number of words in the English translation that demonstrate again a laziness in putting exactly what St. Thomas has said in the Latin. For instance, *rerum* is translated not "of things" but "of the world", *aliqua* as "things" instead of "some things" and *cognitione* not as "knowledge" but as "intelligence". However, over-all the mistranslations do not affect the understanding of the passage.

The argument rests basically on the fact/effect that some things demonstrate an order to end even though they are obviously not aware of either the end or the order to which they are subject. This applies to all natural things insofar as the act naturally and not intelligently. The principle is that nothing is ordered to an end except by an intellect that knows the end and intends it. Clearly it is not anyone of human intelligence that is in control of nature. Accordingly there must be an intelligence that directs natural operations to their ends that is higher than human intellect. That is what we call God. St. Thomas uses the example of the arrow travelling to its target because of a direction in the arrow that plainly comes from the archer and not from any knowledge in the arrow.

A superhuman intelligence need not of course be God. It could be an angel. Hence there are a couple of gaps to fill in. But St. Thomas does not deem it necessary to elaborate in this regard. For we know that every spiritual being other than God is not superior to the human soul to such an extent that it can control its end. It has no dominance over the human will. All beings of spiritual form in fact have the same natural end, if able to attain it at different levels.

St. Thomas has repeated this proof in the Prologue to his commentary on the Gospel of St. John. It may be noticed that he calls it the most efficacious way. It is confirmed in moral terms by the testimony of conscience.

Quidam enim per auctoritatem Dei in ipsius cognitionem pervenerunt; et haec est via efficacissima. Videmus enim ea quae sunt in

rebus naturalibus, propter finem agere, et consequi utiles et certos
fines; et cum intellectu careant, se ipsa dirigere non possunt, nisi ab
aliquo dirigente per intellectum dirigantur et moveantur. Et hinc est
quod ipse motus rerum naturalium in finem certum, indicat esse al-
iquid altius, quo naturales res diriguntur in finem et gubernantur. Et
ideo cum totus cursus naturae ordinate in finem procedat et diriga-
tur, de necessitate oportet nos ponere aliquid altius, quod dirigat ista
et sicut dominus gubernet: et hic est Deus.

"3 Some attained to a knowledge of God through his authority,
and this is the most efficacious way. For we see the things in nature
acting for an end, and attaining to ends which are both useful and
certain. And since they lack intelligence, they are unable to direct
themselves, but must be directed and moved by one directing them,
and who possesses an intellect. Thus it is that the movement of the
things of nature toward a certain end indicates the existence of
something higher by which the things of nature are directed to an
end and governed. And so, since the whole course of nature advances to an end in an orderly way and is directed, we have to posit
something higher which directs and governs them as Lord; and this
is God."

Aristotle will prove in Metaphysics XII that God is the final cause
of all beings other than God. Yet his treatment in this regard seems
to puzzle modern interpreters. For the focus is on God as an object
of desire. This is complicated by bringing in the problem of how
something can be an unmoved mover, which is what has earlier
been established about God as the first mover. It is clear that as an
object of desire (and knowledge) one can move another without being moved oneself. But this then seems to exclude positing God as

the first efficient cause of motion. Must not any mover change in causing motion? Moreover, what is in motion naturally supposes that it has been moved and will be moved. It is the act of what is potential as it is potential, so a state of potency has to precede its act. How can there be a first motion that is not a passage from a previous state of potency?

This problem is not resolved without making a distinction between efficient cause and moving cause, something that is not always clear in Aristotle. The first or unmoved "mover" (it cannot be a natural/physical agent) does not cause by causing motion but by creating the form in matter (bodily substance) that then has to operate by way of motion. The first man for instance was not moved to be (i.e. generated) but generation only occurred with regard to subsequent human beings. Motion strictly speaking is accidental action that requires the subject to be in potency before the action. But even substantial change or mutation requires there be matter out of which the new bodily form is educed. The first "mover" therefore has to create both the form and matter that belongs to the natural thing or body. Thereafter all activity has to come out of matter by eduction from matter by the moving cause. Beethoven's musical productions thus already were potentially in him years before he began to compose.

God therefore is first efficient cause as creator as well as being the supreme exemplary cause or extrinsic formal cause and most desirable object or final cause of all things other than God. God being an intelligence, things come into being only pursuant to his absolutely free will and so far as things in matter are concerned bodily reality comes into existence by con-creation of form and matter.

Hence, at the beginning of lesson 12 of Book 12 St. Thomas says: "2627. Having shown how the first mover is both an intelligence and an intelligible object, here the Philosopher aims to investigate how the first mover is a good and an object of desire; and in regard to this he does two things. First (1102:C 2628), he shows how the good is present in the universe, according to his opinion; and second (1105:C 2638), according to the opinions of other philosophers ("And we must not fail")."

The universe referred to includes not only the physical universe but also the spiritual order of reality, that is everything that has to come into existence by divine creation, manifested in the threefold causality whereby God's existence is proved. But the focus in this last part of Book 12 is on final causality, which involves the consideration of the order of the universe. This order however has two aspects not only in relation to God as the extrinsic end but also in the interrelation between the parts of the universe as its intrinsic good which is ordered to the extrinsic good.

Thus St, Thomas comments: "2629. He accordingly says, first (1103), that the universe has its good and end in both ways. For there is a separate good, which is the first mover, on which the heavens and the whole of nature depend as their end or desirable good, as has been shown (1067:C 2520. And since all things having one end must agree in their ordination to that end, some order must be found in the parts of the universe; and so the universe has both a separate good and a good of order."

He continues: "In this way too the separate good of the universe, which is the first mover, is a greater good than the good of order which is found in the universe. For the whole order of the universe

exists for the sake of the first mover inasmuch as the things contained in the mind and will of the first mover are realized in the ordered universe. Hence the whole order of the universe must depend
on the first mover." (2631).

Within the internal order the lower is for the sake of the higher:
"2632. Here he shows the ways in which the parts of the universe
contribute to its order. He says that all things in the universe are
ordered together in some way, but not all are ordered alike, for example, sea animals, birds, and plants. Yet even though they are not
ordered in the same way, they are still not disposed in such a way
that one of them has no connection with another; but there is some
affinity and relationship of one with another. For plants exist for the
sake of animals, and animals for the sake of men. That all things are
related to each other is evident from the fact that all are connected
together to one end."

How things without knowledge are ordered has been part of the
proof of an intelligent orderer: "Now the nature of each thing is a
kind of inclination implanted in it by the first mover, who directs it
to its proper end; and from this it is clear that natural beings act for
the sake of an end even though they do not know that end, because
they acquire their inclination to their end from the first intelligence." (2634)

Then St. Thomas explains the influence of chance or accidental
factors in the material order of things: "2637. The answer briefly
stated, then, is that order requires two things: a distinction between
the things ordered, and the contribution of the distinct things to the
whole. As regard the first of these, order is found in all things without fail; but as regards the second, order is found in some things,

and these are the things which are highest and closest to the first principle, as the separate substances and the heavenly bodies, in which there is no element of chance or anything contrary to their nature. But order is lacking in some things, namely, in [lower] bodies, which are sometimes subject to chance and to things which are contrary to their nature. This is so because of their distance from the first principle, which is always the same."

The fifth way argues then for one supreme ruler of the whole universe. Amongst intelligent creatures a similar order has to be in place in so far as God orders these highest being through their own free wills, which demands that they rule themselves and their subjects, in the various natural and institutional societies, in accordance with their understanding and consciousness of the divinely constituted moral law.

Thus St. Thomas concludes his commentary on the Metaphysics: "Hence it follows that the whole universe is like one principality and one kingdom, and must therefore be governed by one ruler. Aristotle's conclusion is that there is one ruler of the whole universe, the first mover, and one first intelligible object, and one first good, whom above he called God (1074:C 2544), who is blessed forever and ever. Amen."

Having completed the five proofs for the existence of God treated of in question 2 we need to go on to St. Thomas's treatment of the essence and attributes of God in the following questions in the *Summa Theologiae*. We should note that the distinction between essence and attributes is not in God but comes from the mode of signification necessarily attached to our mind since we have to draw our knowledge of God from his effects. We may also note that these following conclusions simply draw out what is had from the five ways.

Part 2

The Essence of God

Chapter 6

Essence of God

Having dealt with the question of the existence of God we move to deal with what we can know of his essence and attributes. We have noted that the distinctions between existence, essence and attributes are taken from our natural understanding that has to deal with objects abstracted from our sense knowledge which as we have seen is on three levels corresponding to the three "degrees of abstraction", namely, the physical, mathematical and metaphysical. The proper level in this subject is metaphysical, but even so we only approach a positive understanding of God in terms of his effects.

The essence of God, so far as we can know it, transcends even all the distinctions at the level of Metaphysics. Indeed, as we shall see, it transcends not only the distinction between substance and accident, but also the most basic distinction between act and potency. It is with respect to the first that we make the distinction between essence and attributes. For essence in its primary sense is the same as substance, and the relevant attributes are taken from the three accidents of a spiritual being, of power, intellect and will.

The most basic division of being (*ens*) as we can know it is into potency and act. This is already of beings other than God for they can be distinguished from the one God and multiplied according as their acts of existence (*esse*) are received in different potencies for existence. It is this fundamental potency that is named essence. It is that form of being whereby they can be. It identifies and limits them

101

in terms of existence. God as we have seen is pure act without limit or potency of any kind and thus strictly speaking is pure *esse* without *essentia*. We shall see however that it is necessary for us to speak of God in terms of his effects and so we are constrained to discuss God in terms of his essence.

But this primary notion of potency as essence immediately gives rise to the division of being (*ens*) into substance and accident. For as Aristotle says the primary notion of essence is substance and it is only secondarily that we speak of the essences of accidents. He notes that we should speak only of substances as beings (*entia per se*) and accidents rather as "of beings". For naturally accidents only exist in substances. But as noted this language about being which is composed of *essentia* and *esse* comes from the language about essence.

It is important to notice from the start the centrality of the notion of essence in our understanding and language despite the fact that essence only exists as a part of the real being with which we are primarily concerned. All the other words equivalent to essence, such as nature, whatness (quiddity), form, etc., are also central to all philosophy and science. We should therefore be fully acquainted with St. Thomas's seminal work *De ente et essentia*.

However, there is a further distinction within essence in terms of act and potency into form and matter that it is critical to be aware of in all human discussions; for it is the focus of our understanding of all reality. There too we need to be aware of the corresponding distinction between substance and accident and of the importance of this distinction for human knowledge that itself is divided into that of the intellect and senses, divided further into external and internal.

But it is the more fundamental application of the distinctions between act and potency and substance and accident that are directly
involved in Metaphysics and accordingly in the discussion of the
essence and attributes of God. For the discussion of the essence and
attributes of God is based in the distinction within being (*ens*) between the act of existence (*esse*) and the potency for that act (*essentia*) that first applies to simple essences or pure forms of being
called spiritual. Though we cannot avoid comparing them to mixed
essences composed of form and matter called bodies, the discussion
has to be directed to the relation immediately within being (*ens*) between the potency for existence (*essentia*) and the act of existence
(*esse*). We might mention here the deplorable practice in English
translation of using the same word "being" for both *ens* and *esse*.
This is calculated to derail the discussion right from the start.

The distinction between substance and accidents arises from the
fact that the potency for "to exist" (*esse*) that is first actuated constitutes the being (*ens*) fully *per se* so that subsequent actuations are
necessarily secondary. Moreover, the first act of such a being constitutes it only in its beginning. Secondary acts of an accidental kind
are required for its full perfection. The created spiritual being needs
at least three accidental essences and *esses* that correspond to the
three kinds of causality. As a being it is ordered to do (efficient
cause), with its act in this regard being preceded by power; as an intellectual being it is ordered further to knowledge (formal cause);
and the form had by way of intellectual knowledge is followed by
the inclination that is will (final cause). These also have two states

ones given the common name of powers and the others called acts of understanding and love.

The unity of these three lines of causation may be seen in the fact that the final and (extrinsic) formal causes are in the efficient cause of the intelligent kind. This is not appreciated by the materialist philosopher and scientist who tend to separate the causalities and indeed think of causality only in terms of the unintelligent efficient (force/energy) and material (mass/particle). That of course prevents such a mind from being able to deal with the spiritual, let alone the divine.

The powers of intellect and will may be listed under qualities. As well there are accidents of relation. It will be found necessary in discussion of God in Sacred Theology to speak in terms of essence and substance but not as distinct from the act of existence (*esse*); and also in terms of relation, not as an accident, nor as really distinct from the "substance" of God that is pure act or *esse*. But these theological questions are outside the scope of reason and philosophy, even Metaphysics.

What we cannot avoid is the further complication of the influence of primary matter in the consideration of the essences of bodies. Besides the distinction within substance between form and matter there are the accidents that belong to bodies by reason of primary matter the first of which is quantity, but extend to the other accidents of time (when), place (where and situs), action and passion and habitus (peculiar to the human body). Being related to act and potency action and passion have an analogous application to the spiritual order of things but those accidents necessarily tied to matter have only a metaphorical application.

The metaphysical discussion of God therefore is confined to that of essence or substance and attributes so understood that they are not really distinct from the one being of pure act or simple *esse*. So it is that the first question St. Thomas deals with is the simplicity of God. For all the proofs for God are based on the lack of any potency at all in his being. Potency is the first condition of things being distinct from God on account of being necessarily composed of the act of existence (be - *esse*) being limited by the potency (can be - *essentia*) in which it is received. The whole discussion is complicated by the fact that our human being which governs the nature of our understanding and desire is partly spiritual and partly material, composed specially of a spiritual soul in a material body.

However, let St. Thomas guide us through the difficulties that therefore attach to the consideration of the essence and attributes of God. The discussion ranges from questions 3 to 26. Questions 3 to 11 concern the essence of God with questions 12 and 13 devoted to problems to do with how we know such essence. Questions 14 to 26 then concern what we call the attributes which are power, intellect and will in terms of what we in our experience know as both potencies and acts but which we have to understand as but aspects of the one divine pure act. We will come to the attributes but we might note here that St. Thomas deals with them in the order of intellect first then will then power.

The notion of power presents some difficulty because of its connotation of potency. St. Thomas makes the distinction between active and passive potency so as to eliminate any notion of potency in any pure sense. But even so the notion of active potency needs some purification to bring out the reference to act that it has in creatures.

It really refers to the "do" that issues from "can do". It tends to be associated with understand in spiritual things though it is clearly distinct from the power of understanding in things below man and in unconscious human bodily powers of operation, such as nutrition. But we will come back to this aspect of the question of power where St. Thomas deals with it.

Coming to the questions relating to essence, St. Thomas has said that we know what God is not rather than what he is. He will allow however that we do have some positive knowledge of God if only indirect and relative. The problem in this regard is that we are naturally oriented to knowing things through knowing their essences or forms of being and these have two relations as noted, one to what is above them, the act of existence or *esse*, to which they are related as potency to act, and the other to what is below them, the pure potency of primary matter, to which they are related as act to potency.

Knowability for us, therefore, is based on the determinateness of form relative to the indeterminateness of matter. But we are aware that the source of this determinacy of form is somehow from act rather than potency and so the higher act of existence to which essence and form are related is unknowable not because of any deficiency in act but rather because of a super sufficiency, rather like the lack of visibility of light as compared with colour.

So it is that in regard to the knowledge of God we do have a sense of something above us and are dazzled as it were with the thought. Indeed, in a rightly disposed person there is little problem in concluding to the existence of God as dealt with in the five ways. The natural disposition is one of awe, humility and gratitude at the gift of existence. However, we know from Revelation that there is a

moral dimension in any thinking that reflects on the sense of freedom belonging to our will. To acknowledge our debt to the creator
is felt to somehow make us less free, which a right moral attitude is
able to put down to the sin of pride. But there are some, prompted
by Lucifer, who would have us believe that pride in human excellence had independently of anything else is a virtue, indeed the most
important of human virtues. In Post-Reformation times it has even
come to be expressed generally in the political philosophy called
Liberalism, which declares the Catholic Church instituted by God as
the main obstacle to human liberty.

However, these are matters discussed elsewhere, though they do
enable us to understand better the difficulties placed in the way of
acknowledging the existence of God, and of discussing his essence
and attributes. We may treat first then of the metaphysical issue of
the essence or substance of God. This focuses on the divine being
(*esse*) about which there are three main considerations, its simplicity
(q. 3), unity (q. 11) and perfection (q. 4). The other considerations
of infinity (q. 7), omnipresence (q. 8), immutability (q. 9), and eternity (q. 10) flow out of these whilst the discussion of goodness (q. 5
& q. 6) is explanatory of that of perfection.

Here we may limit our comment to the three main considerations. That God is simple (*sine plex* – without fold) is evident from
all five ways and most evident from the third. For complexity or
compositeness is the mark of an effect, which is an existent whose
act of existence (*esse* – be) is received in and limited by its essence
(*essentia* – can be). This kind of existent with an essence in the primary sense of substance is then further composed of accidents as
indicated. This complexity is further complicated where the essenc-

es themselves are composite, composed both in the substance having substantial form and primary matter and then having many more accidents needed to complete its entity.

The materialist scientist, such as Richard Dawkins, cannot raise his mind above the level of bodies whose perfection requires the most complexity, and the more perfect its level of being the more complex it is. So Dawkins is troubled by the thought of God having to be the most complex of beings if he is to be held to be the creator of all things. Then he quite foolishly asks the question of the child: "then who made God?" In being pure act or simple *esse* God has all the actual perfections that it is possible to have. But in having no understanding of the distinction between potency and act the level of the materialists' thinking descends to the lowest level of potency in primary matter, where it is then conceived/ imagined as secondary matter at the lowest level of bodily actuality.

The quantitative property of body brings in the mathematical imagination which tends to govern the scientists' thinking especially as we have explained through the contraction of the notion of science to that of the mixed or medial physico-mathematics since Newton. The dominance of Mathematics here affects the understanding of Logic itself with the result of every concept being reduced to a univocal level. In some way then "matter" becomes the most general genus of all modern thinking out of which "evolves" all the differences of things.

St. Thomas finds it necessary to go through the various kinds of potency, real and logical. But the basic article in question 3 is article 4: "Whether existence and essence are the same in God?" This is most clearly shown in the third way where essence as potency to existence indicates only what can exist. This shows that if it does exist it is a composite being. Only what has the act of existence pure and simple is not an effect and requires no causal explanation.

From the simplicity of God follows his unity. This is dealt with in question 11. What is simple is necessarily one though what is one is not necessarily simple. For besides God every composite being has unity and unity can be found in beings of much complexity.

One (*unum*) indeed is a transcendental mode of being (*ens*). Primarily it belongs to substance or *ens per se,* but a composite being is not able to operate except with and through its necessary accidents. Spiritual beings then operate through spiritual powers of which intellect and will are the two distinctive kinds following forms had by way of spiritual knowledge. But there is question of powers and acts issuing from the very fact that they are spiritual beings. We will discuss these when we come to power in question 25. We shall also see that question 18 has relevance to this consideration of powers and acts.

Material beings or bodies however have a greater degree of complexity because of the composition of their essences into form and matter. Thus there is a twofold reason of complexity, with the need for many forms to complete the greater influence of primary matter. In this regard the higher forms of material being are more complex for the sake of a higher degree of unity, so that living bodies are more complex than non-living, animals than plants. Thus human nature is the most complex of bodies having life on three levels, vegetative, animal, and properly human.

On the other hand, the more elementary forms of bodies have a complexity of a more indeterminate kind and hence are less unified, being closer to the indeterminacy of primary matter. This makes them more difficult to understand not because of their complexity as such but because of their tendency to change forms easily. This brings in a distinction between two notions of unity, the formal or transcendental notion referred to which applies to all essences as forms of being and the predicamental notion of unity that applies to material individuals within specific forms of bodies.

This latter notion is based in quantity as the first property of a body by reason of its matter and it is specially the object of bodies at the second or mathematical degree of abstraction. It is the confusion of these two opposed notions of unity that Aristotle criticised in Plato, evidently coming from the influence of Pythagoras in his thinking. Because of the dominance of Mathematics (from the influence of Descartes, Kant and Newton) in the modern notion of science practically all modern philosophy and science is unable to rise above this mathematical/logical level to the metaphysical transcendental level not only in regard to unity but also in regard to being itself and all its transcendental modes.

In article 4 of question 11 St. Thomas points out that God is not only supremely being because pure act but also supremely one because absolutely simple *esse* and thus most undivided of all. This absolute transcendental unity is not relativised by the trinity of persons but they flow from it so that it is not possible for the one God to exist in any other way. This super-transcendental threefold personhood of God is furthrest removed from any material/quantitative notion of predicamental multitude. A similar distance from potency when considering the attributes of God will be noted in considering below the power of God. For it too must be based in *esse* pure and simple.

In question 4 St. Thomas deals with the notion of perfection in God. That God is absolutely perfect in being and contains all perfection is evident from the fact that he is simple *esse*. However the notion of perfection, like all other notions applied to God, comes first from his effects where it means "thoroughly made". Since all creatures are composite it is possible for them to lack some act, which they necessarily do in relation to other beings but which they can also lack in relation to what is due to them. The former connotes imperfection but not necessarily something evil in them; evil is lack of a due good. So a stone that does not have sight is not as perfect as an animal that does; it is called sightless but it is not for that called blind.

The transcendental notion of good is connected with that of perfect. Dionysius states that the good is from an integrating cause; whilst evil is from whatsoever defect. Thus it is related to the notion of whole and even holy. Everything is good in so far as it has being. Lack of goodness comes from lack of being in some respect, as the blind lacks sight that is due.

All the other questions regarding the essence of God treated by St. Thomas follow from these three main ones. They are questions 7, 8, 9 & 10. However, we will only comment shortly on them. The infinite is that which lacks limit. With regard to infinity we just need to note the distinction between actual and potential infinity. Primary matter and such things that flow from it, such as quantity considered as such, are infinite because form is what determines them. God is called infinite actually because he lacks nothing.

Being the cause in giving the act of existence (*esse*) to all things other than God he is connected most intimately to them as effects. All other causes are secondary, determining existence of others under God according to the difference of their forms of being. It is through secondary or natural causes that God brings others into existence. We will say more about this when we come to discuss the power of God.

The immutability and eternity of God also follow the simplicity unity and perfection of the pure act of *esse*. But we are constrained to express them in terms of absolute opposition to motion and time. The notion of *aevum,* which is a form of duration that transcends motion and time strictly taken, is nonetheless only relatively opposed to that of time. It can be given special treatment when dealing with pure spirits or angels. Human beings exist in both lives of duration, and as we know from Revelation beings of spiritual form will share by grace in the divine eternal life.

Before turning to consider the attributes of God, which he deals with in questions 14 to 26, St. Thomas considers two questions, 12 & 13: How God is known to us, and the Names of God. As to the first question the main articles are 1, 4 &5.

In article 1 St. Thomas says that though God is the most intelligible and knowable of all things his being may not be knowable not by reason of any deficiency in the object but on account of a deficiency in the knower, or excess on the part of the object, just as the owl is only able to see in the weakest light. So some have argued that no created intellect can see the essence of God. His response is set out below.

Hoc igitur attendentes, quidam posuerunt quod nullus intellectus creatus essentiam Dei videre potest.Sed hoc inconvenienter dicitur. Cum enim ultima hominis beatitudo in altissima eius operatione consistat, quae est operatio intellectus, si nunquam essentiam Dei videre potest intellectus creatus, vel nunquam beatitudinem obtinebit, vel in alio eius beatitudo consistet quam in Deo. Quod est alienum a fide. In ipso enim est ultima perfectio rationalis creaturae, quia est ei principium essendi, intantum enim unumquodque perfectum est, inquantum ad suum principium attingit. Similiter etiam est praeter rationem. Inest enim homini naturale desiderium cognoscendi causam, cum intuetur effectum; et ex hoc admiratio in hominibus consurgit. Si igitur intellectus rationalis creaturae pertingere non possit ad primam causam rerum, remanebit inane desiderium naturae.

"Therefore some who considered this, held that no created intellect can see the essence of God. This opinion, however, is not tenable. For as the ultimate beatitude of man consists in the use of his highest function, which is the operation of his intellect; if we suppose that the created intellect could never see God, it would either never attain to beatitude, or its beatitude would consist in something else beside God; which is opposed to faith. For the ultimate perfection of the rational creature is to be found in that which is the principle of its being; since a thing is perfect so far as it attains to its principle. Further the same opinion is also against reason. For there resides in every man a natural desire to know the cause of any effect which he sees; and thence arises wonder in men. But if the intellect of the rational creature could not reach so far as to the first cause of things, the natural desire would remain void."

This response has led however to much controversy not with regard to what is said about the knowledge of God from Faith, but from reason. For St. Thomas seems to be saying that we can prove not only from Faith but also from reason that the created intellect can know the essence of God as he is in himself. That would mean that we would not need to know Revelation in order to be certain of being able to obtain the beatific vision.

We cannot go into the problem that arises from this here but have dealt with it elsewhere. Our opinion is that it cannot be that we can know from reason alone that the created intellect is even capable of the happiness accorded by grace just as it is not possible by reason alone to know of the possibility of God being a Trinity of persons. For this knowledge is supernatural, above reason altogether, and only able to be had by the help of grace. St. Thomas's argument seems only to prove that we can know the essence of God as cause and therefore naturally only in terms of his effects, as has been posited all along up to this point.

Nonetheless, the way the argument is put certainly seems to have it go further. But the resolution of the problem of interpretation in our opinion may be had by reference to the way St. Thomas himself says we may use reason in theology when dealing with the Trinity in q. 32, art. 1 ad 2: "Reason may be employed in two ways to establish a point: firstly, for the purpose of furnishing sufficient proof of some principle, as in natural science, where sufficient proof can be brought to show that the movement of the heavens is always of uniform velocity. Reason is employed in another way, not as furnishing a sufficient proof of a principle, but as confirming an already established principle, by showing the congruity of its results, as in astrology the theory of eccentrics and epicycles is considered as established, because thereby the sensible appearances of the heavenly movements can be explained; not, however, as if this proof were sufficient, forasmuch as some other theory might explain them. In the first way, we can prove that God is one; and the like. In the second way, reasons avail to prove the Trinity; as, when assumed to be true, such reasons confirm it. We must not, however, think that the trinity of persons is adequately proved by such reasons. This becomes evident when we consider each point; for the infinite goodness of God is manifested also in creation, because to produce from nothing is an act of infinite power. For if God communicates Himself by His infinite goodness, it is not necessary that an infinite effect should proceed from God: but that according to its own mode and capacity it should receive the divine goodness. Likewise, when it is said that joyous possession of good requires partnership, this holds in the case of one not having perfect goodness: hence it needs to share some other's good, in order to have the goodness of complete happiness. Nor is the image in our mind an adequate proof in the case of God, forasmuch as the intellect is not in God and ourselves univocally. Hence, Augustine says (Tract. xxvii. in Joan.) that by faith we arrive at knowledge, and not conversely."

Knowing therefore that our happiness or beatitude consists in the beatific vision – which necessarily includes knowledge of the Trinity – we can by reason confirm this as conformable with the natural desire to know fully God as cause of the created effects from which we can naturally know his existence and other aspects of his essence such as simplicity, unity and absolute perfection.

This position is reinforced by what St. Thomas says in the body of the response to Article 1, which concludes with a warning against attempting to prove by reason what is knowable only by Faith: "*I answer that* It is impossible to attain to the knowledge of the Trinity by natural reason. For, as above explained (Question [12], Articles [4], [12]), man cannot obtain the knowledge of God by natural reason except from creatures. Now creatures lead us to the knowledge of God, as effects do to their cause. Accordingly, by natural reason we can know of God that only which of necessity belongs to Him as the principle of things, and we have cited this fundamental principle in treating of God as above (Question 12, Article [12]). Now, the creative power of God is common to the whole Trinity; and hence it belongs to the unity of the essence, and not to the distinction of the persons. Therefore, by natural reason we can know what belongs to the unity of the essence, but not what belongs to the distinction of the persons. Whoever, then, tries to prove the trinity of persons by natural reason, derogates from faith in two ways. Firstly, as regards the dignity of faith itself, which consists in its being concerned with invisible things, that exceed human reason; wherefore the Apostle says that 'faith is of things that appear not' (Heb. 11:1), and the same Apostle says also, 'We speak wisdom among the perfect, but not the wisdom of this world, nor of the princes of this world; but we speak the wisdom of God in a mystery which is hidden' (1 Cor. 2: 6-7). Secondly, as regards the utility of drawing others to the faith. For when anyone in the endeavour to prove the faith brings forward reasons which are not cogent, he falls under the ridicule of the unbelievers: since they suppose that we stand upon such reasons, and that we believe on such grounds.

Therefore, we must not attempt to prove what is of faith, except by authority alone, to those who receive the authority; while as regards others it suffices to prove that what faith teaches is not impossible. Hence it is said by Dionysius (Div. Nom. ii): 'Whoever wholly resists the word, is far off from our philosophy; whereas if he regards the truth of the word' — i.e. 'the sacred word, we too follow this rule'."

Articles 4 and 5 further reinforce the same point about the need for a divine elevation by grace even to have the possibility of seeing the essence of God in the beatific vision. As for positing a natural desire in us for this supernatural happiness, since it is known to be naturally impossible there would seem to be no rational basis for such a desire prior to the reception of grace. However, we will not go any further into this question here.

Moving on to question 13, "The Names of God", there are 12 articles. In the first article St. Thomas explains how we can know the essence of God but only according to the limits of our understanding of things. Basically, this means that the names we can give to God come from the names we give to creatures. This results in certain conditions attaching to the names, that mean to refer to the natures of things as real, say, substance, or good, but are inevitably conditioned by reason not only of their composite character, being the substance "of", or goodness "in" a subject, but also of having to conform to the mode of human understanding because of having to abstract essences to which the mind attaches logical relations such as universality and also treats of concepts at different levels of abstraction, so as to distinguish even at the conceptual level between "abstract" concepts, such as "humanity" from "concrete" concepts, such as "man".

There is a fair bit in this but it is better to read the articles concerned. Some idea of the distinctions needed can be gathered from St. Thomas's reply to objection 2 of article 1: "Because we know and name God from creatures, the names we attribute to God signify what belongs to material creatures, of which the knowledge is natural to us. And because in creatures of this kind what is perfect and subsistent is compound; whereas their form is not a complete subsisting thing, but rather is that whereby a thing is; hence it follows that all names used by us to signify a complete subsisting thing must have a concrete meaning as applicable to compound things; whereas names given to signify simple forms, signify a thing not as subsisting, but as that whereby a thing is; as, for instance, whiteness signifies that whereby a thing is white. And as God is simple, and subsisting, we attribute to Him abstract names to signify His simplicity, and concrete names to signify His substance and perfection, although both these kinds of names fail to express His mode of being, forasmuch as our intellect does not know Him in this life as He is".

All this affects how we speak of God, or the different kinds of names we use. Thus, we have St. Thomas explaining in articles 2, 3 and 4 how the names we use can refer to God's substance, how some can be taken "literally" and others "metaphorically" (this difference not always corresponding to how we use it in modern linguistic parlance – this causing a lot of confusion and even misinterpretation in following St Thomas's argumentation), and how the difference in names, though necessarily referring to one and the same God, are not for that synonymous because of the difference of concepts.

But in articles 5 to 10 St. Thomas addresses the central question of the analogy of the names we apply to God, repeating Aristotle's distinction between univocal, equivocal and analogous names. Here we have to be rather careful because Aristotle uses terminology that for one thing calls what is analogous equivocal, so that later scholastics had to invent the distinction between analogy "by design" (true analogy) and analogy "by accident" (equivocal).

St. Thomas will refer to this in his reply to objection 4 in article 10: "The term 'animal' applied to a true and a pictured animal is not purely equivocal; for the Philosopher takes equivocal names in a large sense, including analogous names; because also being, which is predicated analogically, is sometimes said to be predicated equivocally of different predicaments." The proper meaning of analogy is difficult to grasp and this is made more difficult because St. Thomas does not have a separate work on analogy (like Cajetan does – which complicates the discussion because he introduces a different terminology) but addresses it to a large degree in answering objections.

For instance, probably the best insight we get is in his answer to objection 5 in article 10: "Neither a Catholic nor a pagan knows the very nature of God as it is in itself; but each one knows it according to some idea of causality, or excellence, or remotion (Question 12, Article [12]). So a pagan can take this name 'God' in the same way when he says an idol is God, as the Catholic does in saying an idol is not God. But if anyone should be quite ignorant of God altogether, he could not even name Him, unless, perhaps, as we use names the meaning of which we know not."

Thus we note there are three bases for analogy, causality, excellence (eminence) and remotion. Excellence can be brought under causality, as extrinsic formal causality (somewhat seen in the notion of proportionality). If opposed to causality this is to the other modes of efficient and final (where we may limit the relation to proportion).

It is the last, remotion, however, that is not so well appreciated, and even left out of the full treatment of analogy or treated as what constitutes the whole notion. But it applies specially where we are dealing with "things" negatively, as in Metaphysics one applies the notion of being to non-being, not because there is any positive or real connection between the two concepts (indeed they are contradictorily opposed) but because our mind is constrained to link "is" with the notion of nothing, or with negations and privations, in order to talk about them, or even think about them.

Aristotle will call use of the copula "is" in a statement or proposition the "is of the proposition" as opposed to the "is" that intends to refer to real existence. But we need to be careful here also because we need to use the "is" of a proposition when we intend to speak of real existence, as when we assert in the conclusion that God exists. This is a matter that has been discussed in regard to question 2, where St. Thomas uses the distinction.

This notion of analogy, which comes from a purely logical extension of our words and concepts has to be kept separate from the other two where there is a real basis for the linking of the two names and concepts, as when we say for instance that God is good, or even that porridge is good and a holy person is good. Even when we say urine is healthy there is a real cause/effect relation underlying the use of the same word (and concept) for two things so essentially opposed.

The basic distinction within the notion of analogy is then between names and concepts that are purely logically connected because of the mode of signification required by the nature of the human intellect, and those that are not so purely logically related, though there still remains a distinction between the things signified and the mode of signification.

Thus we can see the same names applied to "god" where the commonness of meaning may in the one case belong to the order of opinion, and in another to the order of reality, or the truth of science as understood by Aristotle and St. Thomas. This is an aspect of the discussion of analogy that has tricked up many, even Thomists of the present day. We are thinking not just of John Finnis in his extension of the meaning of law "by analogy" to an unjust law, but also of Ralph McInerny who apparently would have it that analogy depends on a purely logical use of words.

These problems, however, belong to a more extensive treatment of analogy than we can give here. It is enough if the distinctions discussed allow us to sort out the distinctions St. Thomas makes between using the name of God for what he truly is, or only according to participation (as used in Scripture), or according to opinion, which latter can stand with the falsity of such opinion if meant to refer to God as he really is, as is brought out in the quote from article 10 above.

This question 13 finishes up with articles 11 and 12. In the first St. Thomas deals with the name revealed to Moses "I am Who am". This is the most proper name of God even though it has the least reference to nature or essence, whereby we need to name anything. This almost absolute exclusion of the mode of our understanding suits most properly what we are trying to name. However, the name "God" in so far as it refers to God as universal principle of being, and universal provider of goodness, has a certain properness from our relation to him.

Finally, in article 12 St. Thomas comes to reaffirm that we can have more than negative knowledge of God, and therefore names can be affirmative, and our concepts or ideas and statements do correspond to and have real reference to what is outside our mind. With this we can move on to deal with what may be called the attributes of God.

Part 3

Attributes of God

Chapter 7

Attributes of God

We have noted above that in regard to the discussion of God it is only spiritual attributes that are relevant. Accordingly, they fall into three categories, of power, intellect and will. St. Thomas deals with these in the order: intellect, will and power. The last needs some special attention because St. Thomas tends to associate it with creation whereas the other two can be considered entirely unrelated to anything other than God; indeed, they come into special focus in the treatment of the Trinity. We will therefore deal with the attributes, contained in questions 14 to 26, in the order that St. Thomas has dealt with them, beginning with God's intellectual life in qq. 14 to 17, where he treats of God's knowledge, and the questions of ideas, truth and falsity in regard to God's knowledge. It is to be noted that we are concerned here only with God as one, not as triune, the treatment of which follows in qq. 27 to 43.

The first thing to notice is that the word St. Thomas uses for knowledge is "science" [Latin *scientia*]. The word science in Latin has a different meaning in modern English where it is associated with intellectual/rational knowledge. But its meaning is narrower than pre-modern usage coming from the ancient Greek and in particular that of Aristotle, which is the meaning which St. Thomas is using. Aristotle used science in a general sense and in a special sense, the first including wisdom or Metaphysics the second opposing it to wisdom and referring principally to the particular sciences of Mathematics and Physics (and the mixed science of physico-mathematics as previously explained).

The modern usage deliberately excludes wisdom or the science of Metaphysics, indeed, it contemptuously rejected it, and so is narrower than science taken as knowledge here by St. Thomas. But it is even narrower than science taken in its traditional particular sense. For since Newton it virtually restricts the notion of science to the medial science of mathematical physics (which comes with a mixed scientific method). More telling still its notion of the physical side of this science is emptied of any natural forms or ends and contracts to a notion interested only in material/efficient causality, called "empirical" or "experimental".

Thus, it is that it is so ridiculously reductionist that it cannot deal properly with the higher forms of nature, life and sense consciousness, let alone the powers and actions of the higher internal senses. Such a notion of knowledge as science is minimally intellectual/rational and totally unfit for use in the discussion in which St. Thomas is engaged regarding the nature and attributes of God. It was so unsuitable in regard to the consideration of the proofs for the existence of God. This is the basic reason behind the inability of the modern mind, including that of well educated Catholics, even schooled to some extent in the thought of Aquinas, to understand the proofs.

Most thus spend their time in presenting "objections" made useless, and at times idiotic, by such distorted notions of knowledge and science. Things are not helped when the ancients and mediaevals sometimes used *scientia* to refer to knowledge in such general terms as even to include sense knowledge. The modern usage itself makes it difficult to distinguish intellectual and rational knowledge from the knowledge of irrational animals. All this is compounded further by poor translations from the Latin.

For instance, where St. Thomas says: *considerandum est quod cognoscentia a non cognoscentibus in hoc distinguuntur, quia non cognoscentia nihil habent nisi formam suam tantum; sed cognoscens natum est habere formam etiam rei alterius, nam species cogniti est in cognoscente,* this is translated "we must note that intelligent beings are distinguished from non-intelligent beings in that the latter possess only their own form; whereas the intelligent being is naturally adapted to have also the form of some other thing; for the idea of the thing known is in the knower".

This is a howler of the first water in the discussion of knowledge. For *cognoscens* means knower (knowing thing), which includes knowing by sense knowledge, not intelligent beings (*intelligens*). How can anyone be expected to follow what St. Thomas is saying in this critically important context if such mistakes are made – and unfortunately most moderns do not read St. Thomas in the original Latin, as is obvious when such bloomers are allowed to go unnoticed and uncorrected for decades?

Is it any wonder that "contributions that more recent research has provided and continues to offer" (modern excuses for "research") in philosophical and theological matters in recent times has turned academics away from true understanding of what St. Thomas has to offer in philosophy to criticisms instead by highly respected commentators of St. Thomas, not just non-Catholic but also Catholic. They show, as Pope St. Paul VI said in *Lumen ecclesiae*: "the kind of innovative daring St Thomas showed in his day, but ...

often lack the clear vision and balance which the great doctor possessed in a supreme degree."

In my view the leading modern authorities on the matter, even
though sincere Catholics, are so affected by their secularist civil education (now having taken over the field of Logic itself) that, either
by way of attraction or reaction, they have incautiously involved
themselves in the problem and succumbed to one or other of the
two dangers that lie, like Scylla and Charybdis (Pope St. Paul VI's
description), on either side of the balanced position. The balanced
position, which St. Thomas possessed "in a supreme degree", is regarded as flawed according to modern logic and science.

Once the proper knowledge to be attributed to God is understood there is no difficulty following what St. Thomas has to say in
all 16 articles of question 14. What he has to say in his preface however we will need to consider more closely when we are dealing with
power.

In question 15 he goes on to treat of ideas in God. That is because in created intellects there are two intellectual acts, of apprehension and judgment, whose products are called concepts or ideas
and statements or propositions respectively. We simply have to note
that there is no real distinction in God whose intellectual life consists in the perfection of understanding in one act (judgment) and
so there is no need for ideas or indeed the product of the third act of
reasoning (logic). Nonetheless, we are constrained to think and
speak about God in terms of his effects.

As to the question of ideas in God the principal problem is to
how God can have the many ideas of things needed to know the
forms of things as specifically different, without this affecting the

absolute simplicity of the divine being. This is resolved in article 2: "Inasmuch as He knows His own essence perfectly, He knows it according to every mode in which it can be known. Now it can be known not only as it is in itself, but as it can be participated in by creatures according to some degree of likeness".

The next question (16) considers the matter of truth, which relates to the product of judgment, statement or proposition. Again this act and product are not really distinct from the simple *esse* or oneness of God. But we need to deal with it by comparison with truth as we know it as conformity between what is in intellect and being, or thought and thing. There are 8 articles but the matter is resolved fundamentally in the first and second. Truth is in the intellect and therefore may be considered in God as "understand, the understand of an understand" (Aristotle's description of God) and not in the mode of understanding proper to human understanding (judgment) by composition and division of statements or propositions.

In the response to the first article St. Thomas gives the classical definitions of truth: "Consequently there are various definitions of truth. Augustine says (De Vera Relig. xxxvi), 'Truth is that whereby is made manifest that which is;' and Hilary says (De Trin. v) that 'Truth makes being clear and evident' and this pertains to truth according as it is in the intellect. As to the truth of things in so far as they are related to the intellect, we have Augustine's definition (De Vera Relig. xxxvi), 'Truth is a supreme likeness without any unlikeness to a principle': also Anselm's definition (De Verit. xii), 'Truth is rightness, perceptible by the mind alone'; for that is right which is in accordance with the principle; also Avicenna's definition (Metaph.

viii, 6), 'The truth of each thing is a property of the essence which is immutably attached to it.' The definition that 'Truth is the equation of thought and thing' is applicable to it under either aspect."

To the question "whether God is truth" in article 5 St. Thomas gives the following answer: "*I answer that,* As said above (Article [1]), truth is found in the intellect according as it apprehends a thing as it is; and in things according as they have being conformable to an intellect. This is to the greatest degree found in God. For His being is not only conformed to His intellect, but it is the very act of His intellect; and His act of understanding is the measure and cause of every other being and of every other intellect, and He Himself is His own existence and act of understanding. Whence it follows not only that truth is in Him, but that He is truth itself, and the sovereign and first truth."

Following on the question of truth in God St. Thomas considers the matter of falsity in question 17. There is no falsity in God but what St. Thomas says here throws considerable light upon our understanding of the notion of falsity. The four articles would be worth quoting in full. However, I will try to summarize what they say.

In article 1, "whether there is falsity in things", St. Thomas says that there is no falsity in things but because truth is in the intellect as related to things, things are said to be false in various ways depending on their relation to the divine intellect or to created intellects. In the former since the relation of things to the divine intellect is like that of an artist to his works things are sometimes called false or untrue because of their failure to conform to the idea of them in the mind of the artist. This however would seem to apply only where there is sin, in that the free will of the creature declines from what God has ordained for it.

When it comes to the human intellect however, we have to distinguish between artificial things and natural ones, since the latter are the cause of truth in the intellect. Thus there are two ways in which things may be called false. St. Thomas puts it thus: "In one way according to the thing signified, and thus a thing is said to be false as being signified or represented by word or thought that is false. In this respect anything can be said to be false as regards any quality not possessed by it; as if we should say that a diameter is a false commensurable thing, as the Philosopher says (Metaph. v, 34)." Regarding the second way he says: "In another way a thing can be called false, by way of cause—and thus a thing is said to be false that naturally begets a false opinion. And whereas it is innate in us to judge things by external appearances, since our knowledge takes its rise from sense, which principally and naturally deals with external accidents, therefore those external accidents, which resemble things other than themselves, are said to be false with respect to those things; thus gall is falsely honey; and tin, false gold."

In article 2 St. Thomas considers whether there is falsity in the senses. The senses do not know truth but truth is said to be in them in so far as they apprehended things truly. This can occur in three ways: "In the first way, primarily and of its own nature, as in sight there is the likeness of colors, and of other sensible objects proper to it. Secondly, of its own nature, though not primarily; as in sight there is the likeness of shape, size, and of other sensible objects common to more than one sense. Thirdly, neither primarily nor of its own nature, but accidentally, as in sight, there is the likeness of a man, not as man, but in so far as it is accidental to the colored object to be a man."

St. Thomas adds: "Sense, then, has no false knowledge about its proper objects, except accidentally and rarely, and then, because of the unsound organ it does not receive the sensible form rightly; just as other passive subjects because of their indisposition receive defectively the impressions of the agent. Hence, for instance, it happens that on account of an unhealthy tongue sweet seems bitter to a sick person. But as to common objects of sense, and accidental objects, even a rightly disposed sense may have a false judgment, because it is referred to them not directly, but accidentally, or as a consequence of being directed to other things."

In article 3 St. Thomas treats specially of the human intellect: whether falsity is in the intellect? Here the response of St. Thomas needs to be set out in full: "*I answer that,* Just as a thing has being by its proper form, so the knowing faculty has knowledge by the likeness of the thing known. Hence, as natural things cannot fall short of the being that belongs to them by their form, but may fall short of accidental or consequent qualities, even as a man may fail to possess two feet, but not fail to be a man; so the faculty of knowing cannot fail in knowledge of the thing with the likeness of which it is informed; but may fail with regard to something consequent upon that form, or accidental thereto. For it has been said (Article [2]) that sight is not deceived in its proper sensible, but about common sensibles that are consequent to that object; or about accidental objects of sense. Now as the sense is directly informed by the likeness of its proper object, so is the intellect by the likeness of the essence of a thing. Hence the intellect is not deceived about the essence of a thing, as neither the sense about its proper object. But in affirming and denying, the intellect may be deceived, by attributing to the thing of which it understands the essence, something which is not consequent upon it, or is opposed to it. For the intellect is in the same position as regards judging of such things, as sense is as to judging of common, or accidental, sensible objects. There is, however, this difference, as before mentioned regarding truth (Question 16, Article [2]), that falsity can exist in the intellect not only because the intellect is conscious of that knowledge, as it is conscious of truth; whereas in sense falsity does not exist as known, as stated above (Article [2])."

To this he adds: "But because falsity of the intellect is concerned essentially only with the composition of the intellect, falsity occurs also accidentally in that operation of the intellect whereby it knows the essence of a thing, in so far as composition of the intellect is mixed up in it. This can take place in two ways. In one way, by the intellect applying to one thing the definition proper to another; as that of a circle to a man. Wherefore the definition of one thing is false of another. In another way, by composing a definition of parts which are mutually exclusive. For thus the definition is not only false of the thing, but false in itself. A definition such as 'a reasonable four-footed animal' would be of this kind, and the intellect false in making it; for such a statement as 'some reasonable animals are four-footed' is false in itself. For this reason the intellect cannot be false in its knowledge of simple essences; but it is either true, or it understands nothing at all."

The problems with regard to falsity relative to the human intellect and the senses can then be resolved if the appropriate distinc-

tions are applied. In article 4 St. Thomas deals with a problem aris-
ing from what Aristotle says: that a true and a false opinion even if
involving a contradiction is only contrarily opposed (cf. *Peri herme-
neias* – end of Book 2). Has he not also said that one cannot deny
the principle of non-contradiction, as Heraclitus did. One may say it
verbally but one cannot think it: "what a person says is not necessarily what he thinks".

Yet St. Thomas will agree that the opposition between opinions,
even contradictory, is contrary: "*I answer that,* True and false are
opposed as contraries, and not, as some have said, as affirmation
and negation". Then he says: **Reply to Objection 1:** "What is in
things is the truth of the thing; but what is apprehended, is the truth
of the intellect, wherein truth primarily resides. Hence the false is
that which is not as apprehended. To apprehend being, and not-
being, implies contrariety; for, as the Philosopher proves (Peri
Herm. ii), the contrary of this statement 'God is good,' is, 'God is
not good'."

The resolution of this apparent problem lies in understanding
the nature of opposition (something that St. Thomas does not ad-
vert to here). What is contradictory is what cannot exist and not exist together absolutely considered. But what is contrary is what cannot exist together in the same subject. So one (subject) person cannot have contrary opinions, but it is possible for opinions that express contradictory beliefs to exist together, in different subjects,
one person and another.

Hence, St. Thomas adds: "**Reply to Objection 3:** Because contraries, and opposites by way of privation, are by nature about one and

the same thing, therefore there is nothing contrary to God, considered in Himself, either with respect to His goodness or His truth, for in His intellect there can be nothing false. But in our apprehension of Him contraries exist, for the false opinion concerning Him is contrary to the true. So idols are called lies, opposed to the divine truth, inasmuch as the false opinion concerning them is contrary to the true opinion of the divine unity."

In question 18 St. Thomas discusses the notion of life in relation to God. For reasons that appear we will discuss this question with the second last one on power (25). So St. Thomas comes to the questions of will in itself (19 to 21) and together with intellect (22 to 24). The discussions in regard to the will of God (19), his love (20), justice and mercy (21) are so rich in content that it is pretty well impossible to summarize it. It should be read in full and I will only make a couple of comments to bring out some points I wish to add.

In his response in article 1 of q. 19 St. says: "There is will in God, as there is intellect: since will follows upon intellect. For, as natural things have actual existence by their form, so the intellect is actually intelligent by its intelligible form. Now everything has this aptitude towards its natural form, that when it has it not, it tends towards it; and when it has it, it is at rest therein. It is the same with every natural perfection, which is a natural good. This aptitude to good in things without knowledge is called natural appetite. Whence also intellectual natures have a like aptitude as apprehended through its intelligible form; so as to rest therein when possessed, and when not possessed to seek to possess it, both of which pertain to the will. Hence in every intellectual being there is will, just as in every sensible being there is animal appetite. And so there must be will in God,

since there is intellect in Him. And as His intellect is His own existence, so is His will."

The reference to natural appetite and its distinction from appetite flowing from intellectual knowledge, which is will, may have
some relevance to the discussion below of power (and the notion of
divine life). It is to be remembered though that all these aspects,
power, intellect and will, of the divine are not really distinct from
the divine *esse* in itself.

The discussions in articles 2 to 10 do not present any matters of
great difficulty in their interpretation so we leave the readers to
study them themselves. We add a few comments, however, to the
following quotes from the last two articles 11 & 12, which deal with
the various manners in which we refer to the divine will.

q. 19, art. 11:"I answer that Some things are said of God in their
strict sense; others by metaphor, as appears from what has been said
before (I:13:3). When certain human passions are predicated of the
Godhead metaphorically, this is done because of a likeness in the
effect. Hence a thing that is in us a sign of some passion, is signified
metaphorically in God under the name of that passion. Thus with us
it is usual for an angry man to punish, so that punishment becomes
an expression of anger. Therefore punishment itself is signified by
the word anger, when anger is attributed to God. In the same way,
what is usually with us an expression of will, is sometimes metaphorically called will in God; just as when anyone lays down a precept, it is a sign that he wishes that precept obeyed. Hence a divine
precept is sometimes called by metaphor the will of God, as in the
words: 'Thy will be done on earth, as it is in heaven' (Matthew 6:10).
There is, however, this difference between will and anger, that anger

is never attributed to God properly, since in its primary meaning it includes passion; whereas will is attributed to Him properly. Therefore in God there are distinguished will in its proper sense, and will as attributed to Him by metaphor. Will in its proper sense is called the will of good pleasure; and will metaphorically taken is the will of expression, inasmuch as the sign itself of will is called will."

This brings out again how our talk about God has to be taken from created effects and purified of any connotations that cannot be applied to God. In the answer to objection 1, St. Thomas explains how these can be called expressions of will rather than intellect. He says: "Knowledge is not the cause of a thing being done, unless through the will. For we do not put into act what we know, unless we will to do so. Accordingly expression is not attributed to knowledge, but to will." Then in the answer to objection 2 he explains even more clearly the dependence of our expressions about God on our usual expressions about will. This he puts this way: "Expressions of will are called divine wills, not as being signs that God wills anything; but because what in us is the usual expression of our will, is called the divine will in God. Thus punishment is not a sign that there is anger in God; but it is called anger in Him, from the fact that it is an expression of anger in ourselves."

All this is further elaborated upon in the body of his response in article 12: "By these signs we name the expression of will by which we are accustomed to show that we will something. A man may show that he wills something, either by himself or by means of another. He may show it by himself, by doing something either directly, or indirectly and accidently. He shows it directly when he works in his own person; in that way the expression of his will is his own working. He shows it indirectly, by not hindering the doing of a thing; for what removes an impediment is called an accidental mover. In this respect the expression is called permission. He declares his will by means of another when he orders another to perform a work, either by insisting upon it as necessary by precept, and by prohibiting its contrary; or by persuasion, which is a part of counsel. Since in these ways the will of man makes itself known, the same five are sometimes denominated with regard to the divine will, as the expression of that will. That precept, counsel, and prohibition are called the will of God is clear from the words of Matthew 6:10: 'Thy will be done on earth as it is in heaven.' That permission and operation are called the will of God is clear from Augustine (Enchiridion 95), who says: 'Nothing is done, unless the Almighty wills it to be done, either by permitting it, or by actually doing it'."

The replies to objections 3 & 4 throw particular light on the relation between the divine will and human will. Thus regarding objection 3 we have: "Rational creatures are masters of their own acts; and for this reason certain special expressions of the divine will are assigned to their acts, inasmuch as God ordains rational creatures to act voluntarily and of themselves. Other creatures act only as moved by the divine operation; therefore only operation and permission are concerned with these."

And in regard to objection 4: "All evil of sin, though happening in many ways, agrees in being out of harmony with the divine will. Hence with regard to evil, only one expression is assigned, that of prohibition. On the other hand, good stands in various relations to the divine goodness, since there are Good deeds without which we cannot attain to the fruition of that goodness, and these are the subject of precept; and there are others by which we attain to it more perfectly, and these are the subject of counsel. Or it may be said that counsel is not only concerned with the obtaining of greater good; but also with the avoiding of lesser evils."

One could not wish for a more complete treatment of the divine will. However, St. Thomas goes on to deal further with the will in its acts and habits. So in question 20 he considers the primary act of will which is love. In human beings there are two kinds of love, intellectual and sensual. Both are about good, but they can be affected by the misuse of free will. In addition, the second can be affected by being followed "free" from the rule of reason. The discussion of love in God has to be purified of any sensual component, as in the will of any spiritual substance. So too with the notion of joy (pleasure/enjoyment) as rest in the movement of the passion of (sensual) love.

It is also difficult to deal with the notion of happiness, which we will come to in question 26, as being exclusively tied to intellect as the good of understanding. But we will deal with that in connection with question 25. There are four articles in question 20 (on love) but the main point is in article 1: Whether love exists in God. This follows obviously from the fact that will exists in God. All that we need to deal with is to dissociate any sensual love in God, as in us, and any need for there to be an "other" for God to be loving.

How this is reconciled with what we understand by love is explained in the reply to objection 3: "An act of love always tends towards two things; to the good that one wills, and to the person for whom one wills it: since to love a person is to wish that person good. Hence, inasmuch as we love ourselves, we wish ourselves good; and, so far as possible, union with that good. So love is called the unitive force, even in God, yet without implying composition; for the good that He wills for Himself, is no other than Himself, Who is good by His essence, as above shown (Question 6, Articles [1] ,[3]). And by the fact that anyone loves another, he wills good to that other. Thus he puts the other, as it were, in the place of himself; and regards the good done to him as done to himself. So far love is a binding force, since it aggregates another to ourselves, and refers his good to our own. And then again the divine love is a binding force, inasmuch as God wills good to others; yet it implies no composition in God."

In q. 21 St. Thomas deals with justice and mercy in God, in four articles, two on justice and two on mercy. Justice being a virtue in the will of a creature is readily identified as in God, not as in us as a virtue but as an aspect of the divine will. But St. Thomas notes that it is not appropriate to think of it in terms of commutative justice but rather of distributive justice. The former is of a part to part whereas the latter is of a whole to the parts, which is more relevant for the relationship God has to creation. Nonetheless, even this comparison has to be purified of any "political" associations, as in human societies.

This comes out in his reply to objection 1: "Certain of the moral virtues are concerned with the passions, as temperance with concupiscence, fortitude with fear and daring, meekness with anger. Such virtues as these can only metaphorically be attributed to God; since, as stated above (Question 20, Article [1]), in God there are no passions; nor a sensitive appetite, which is, as the Philosopher says (Ethic. iii, 10), the subject of those virtues. On the other hand, cer-

tain moral virtues are concerned with works of giving and expend-
ing; such as justice, liberality, and magnificence; and these reside
not in the sensitive faculty, but in the will. Hence, there is nothing to
prevent our attributing these virtues to God; although not in civil
matters, but in such acts as are not unbecoming to Him. For, as the
Philosopher says (Ethic. x, 8), it would be absurd to praise God for
His political virtues."

In article 2 St. Thomas deals with the question: Whether the justice of God is truth? In view of the depth of insight that his answer
gives in the body and answer to the first objection of the article both
are set out in full.

"Truth consists in the equation of mind and thing, as said above
(Question 16, Article [1]). Now the mind, that is the cause of the
thing, is related to it as its rule and measure; whereas the converse is
the case with the mind that receives its knowledge from things.
When therefore things are the measure and rule of the mind, truth
consists in the equation of the mind to the thing, as happens in ourselves. For according as a thing is, or is not, our thoughts or our
words about it are true or false. But when the mind is the rule or
measure of things, truth consists in the equation of the thing to the
mind; just as the work of an artist is said to be true, when it is in accordance with his art.

Now as works of art are related to art, so are works of justice related to the law with which they accord. Therefore God's justice,
which establishes things in the order conformable to the rule of His
wisdom, which is the law of His justice, is suitably called truth. Thus
we also in human affairs speak of the truth of justice."

"Justice, as to the law that governs, resides in the reason or intellect; but as to the command whereby our actions are governed according to the law, it resides in the will."

Then moving on to articles 3 & 4 St. Thomas deals with mercy as an attribute of God. Here we come to a subject that is so sublime in relation to God that I hesitate to add anything by way of comment. All I will note is that it has both natural and supernatural features that are difficult to separate, with it being here associated with the natural moral virtue of justice and elsewhere, in II-II 30, with the discussion of the theological virtue of charity. The theological virtue of hope may also be brought into the discussion.

St. Thomas sums up the notion of mercy in his response to article 3: "Whether mercy is a virtue", in question 30 of II-II of the Summa: "Mercy signifies grief for another's distress. Now this grief may denote, in one way, a movement of the sensitive appetite, in which case mercy is not a virtue but a passion; whereas, in another way, it may denote a movement of the intellective appetite, in as much as one person's evil is displeasing to another. This movement may be ruled in accordance with reason, and in accordance with this movement regulated by reason, the movement of the lower appetite may be regulated. Hence Augustine says (De Civ. Dei ix, 5) that 'this movement of the mind' (viz. mercy) 'obeys the reason, when mercy is vouchsafed in such a way that justice is safeguarded, whether we give to the needy or forgive the repentant.' And since it is essential to human virtue that the movements of the soul should be regulated by reason, as was shown above (FS, question 59, Articles [4], [5]), it follows that mercy is a virtue."

Mercy then comes out of love, and accordingly belongs to the will in spiritual creatures. But in II-II 30 St. Thomas is dealing with it in regard to the supernatural virtue of Charity, that is, the love of God that follows Faith and Hope. He will explain that it is distinct from Charity because it denotes a relation of a superior to an inferior and that in God it is the highest aspect of the divine goodness and love with respect to creatures. In human beings, however, it is Charity that is the highest virtue because it directly respects God. But we must leave that consideration of mercy to Moral Theology. Here St. Thomas is dealing with mercy in the context of the natural virtue of justice.

So in article 3 of question 21 of the first part of the Summa, with regard to the question: Whether there is mercy in God, he says: "Mercy is especially to be attributed to God, as seen in its effect, but not as an affection of passion. In proof of which it must be considered that a person is said to be merciful [misericors], as being, so to speak, sorrowful at heart [miserum cor]; being affected with sorrow at the misery of another as though it were his own. Hence it follows that he endeavours to dispel the misery of this other, as if it were his; and this is the effect of mercy. To sorrow, therefore, over the misery of others belongs not to God; but it does most properly belong to Him to dispel that misery, whatever be the defect we call by that name. Now defects are not removed, except by the perfection of some kind of goodness; and the primary source of goodness is God, as shown above (I: 6:4). It must, however, be considered that to bestow perfections appertains not only to the divine goodness, but also to His justice, liberality, and mercy; yet under different aspects. The communicating of perfections, absolutely considered, apper-

tains to goodness, as shown above (I: 6:1and I: 6:4); in so far as perfections are given to things in proportion, the bestowal of them belongs to justice, as has been already said (Articles 1); in so far as God
does not bestow them for His own use, but only on account of His
goodness, it belongs to liberality; in so far as perfections given to
things by God expel defects, it belongs to mercy."

How mercy is related to forgiveness is brought out in the reply to
objection 2: "God acts mercifully, not indeed by going against His
justice, but by doing something more than justice; thus a man who
pays another two hundred pieces of money, though owing him only
one hundred, does nothing against justice, but acts liberally or mercifully. The case is the same with one who pardons an offence
committed against him, for in remitting it he may be said to bestow
a gift. Hence the Apostle calls remission a forgiving: 'Forgive one
another, as Christ has forgiven you' (Eph 4:32). Hence it is clear that
mercy does not destroy justice, but in a sense is the fullness thereof.
And thus it is said: 'Mercy exalteth itself above judgement' (James
2:13)."

Forgiveness however (in justice) depends upon true repentance
as is seen in the quote from St. Augustine above. There is a proportion between the offense, repentance and mercy such that no matter
how grave the sin one can hope for God's mercy and forgiveness if
one's repentance (which comes from God given love) is proportionate. We see this in the great sinners who became great saints such as
David and Augustine himself. Indeed, it is of St. Mary Magdalene in
tears (one of the greatest saints) that St. Luke (7: 46) reports Our
Lord's words: "Wherefore I say to thee: Many sins are forgiven her,

because she has loved much. But to whom less is forgiven, he loves less."

One can however presume upon God's mercy and hope for salvation without the need to repent. St. Thomas will deal with the sin of presumption in the context of the theological virtue of hope (not to be confused with the passion of hope). Though this is properly a matter for consideration to do with Faith and therefore within Sacred Theology, St. Thomas brings in considerations that pertain to philosophy or Reason. So we will take a couple of quotes to bring these out.

In II-II q. 21, article 1 he says: "Presumption seems to imply immoderate hope. Now the object of hope is an arduous possible good: and a thing is possible to a man in two ways: first by his own power; secondly, by the power of God alone. With regard to either hope there may be presumption owing to lack of moderation. As to the hope whereby a man relies on his own power, there is presumption if he tends to a good as though it were possible to him, whereas it surpasses his powers, according to Judith 6:15: 'Thou humblest them that presume of themselves.' This presumption is contrary to the virtue of magnanimity which holds to the mean in this kind of hope.

But as to the hope whereby a man relies on the power of God, there may be presumption through immoderation, in the fact that a man tends to some good as though it were possible by the power and mercy of God, whereas it is not possible, for instance, if a man hope to obtain pardon without repenting, or glory without merits."

In article 2 he adds: "As stated above (II-II:20:1) with regard to despair, every appetitive movement that is conformed to a false intellect, is evil in itself and sinful. Now presumption is an appetitive movement, since it denotes an inordinate hope. Moreover it is conformed to a false intellect, just as despair is: for just as it is false that God does not pardon the repentant, or that He does not turn sinners to repentance, so is it false that He grants forgiveness to those who persevere in their sins, and that He gives glory to those who cease from good works: and it is to this estimate that the movement of presumption is conformed."

He goes on to say: "Consequently presumption is a sin, but less grave than despair, since, on account of His infinite goodness, it is more proper to God to have mercy and to spare, than to punish: for the former becomes God in Himself, the latter becomes Him by reason of our sins." It may be noted that in the first article he had said: "This presumption is, properly, the sin against the Holy Ghost, because, to wit, by presuming thus a man removes or despises the assistance of the Holy Spirit, whereby he is withdrawn from sin." But we cannot resolve the apparent problem of gravity here. This would require a consideration of what St. Thomas says in II-II q. 14, which is well beyond the scope of philosophy.

But because of the topicality of the question in relation to the present religious climate as it relates to morals we make a couple of comments. In his book on the theological virtues, Josef Pieper (Ch. 4) entitled "Anticipation of Fulfillment (Presumption)" makes the point that Protestant theology is marked by the adoption of a moral position of presumption. He is careful however to point out that he is speaking objectively and not to be taken as referring to any such sin on the part of an individual. Thus he says: "It is but proper to emphasise at this point what is surely obvious: that we are speaking here only of the objective erroneousness of the presumption that is part of Reformation theology. It would be ridiculous and absurd to raise or attempt to answer the question of subjective guilt."

There appears to be a temptation in some modern Catholic theologians, in their efforts to be "ecumenical", to adopt a similar view. The two errors involved, despair and presumption, are clearly explained above by St. Thomas and we need to be careful not to risk falling into one of the two extremes by reason of wanting to avoid the other.

Generally, the problem applying very much to the present times is the lack of balance described by Pope St. Paul VI in *Lumen ecclesiae,* para. 8: "At this point, however, a serious problem arises: that of finding a new way of conceiving the relationship between faith and reason, or, to state the problem in its most general form, the relationship between the whole created order and the order of religious truth and especially of the Christian message.

In this matter there is evident danger of falling into either of two opposite errors: a *naturalism* which completely eliminates God from the world and especially from Man's life, and a false *supernaturalism,* or *fideism,* which seeks to avoid any doctrinal or spiritual decline by using the principle of authority to suppress the legitimate demands of reason and the development of the natural order. In fideism, however, the principle of authority is extended beyond its proper sphere, namely, the truths of faith revealed by Christ which are the seeds in us of the life to come and which completely transcend the limits of the human intellect.

These two dangers have often arisen throughout the centuries, both before and after St Thomas's time. In our own day they wait,

like Scylla and Charybdis, for those who incautiously involve themselves in the many problems raised by the relations between faith
and reason. In thus involving themselves, men may be showing the
kind of innovative daring St Thomas showed in his day, but they
often lack the clear vision and balance which the great doctor possessed in a supreme degree."

We may connect despair with naturalism or secularism and presumption with supernaturalism or fideism. However, we need to
return to the philosophical level of the discussion even in regard to
mercy in God. In article 4 St. Thomas discusses the question:
Whether in every work of God there are mercy and justice. It is sufficient for our purposes just to quote part of his response in the
body of the article and his answer to objection 1.

"Mercy and truth are necessarily found in all God's works, if
mercy be taken to mean the removal of any kind of defect. Not every defect, however, can properly be called a misery; but only defect
in a rational nature whose lot is to be happy; for misery is opposed
to happiness. For this necessity there is a reason, because since a
debt paid according to the divine justice is one due either to God, or
to some creature, neither the one nor the other can be lacking in any
work of God: because God can do nothing that is not in accord with
His wisdom and goodness; and it is in this sense, as we have said,
that anything is due to God. Likewise, whatever is done by Him in
created things, is done according to proper order and proportion
wherein consists the idea of justice. Thus justice must exist in all
God's works. Now the work of divine justice always presupposes the
work of mercy; and is founded thereupon."

Reply to Obj. 1."Certain works are attributed to justice, and certain others to mercy, because in some justice appears more forcibly and in others mercy. Even in the damnation of the reprobate mercy is seen, which, though it does not totally remit, yet somewhat alleviates, in punishing short of what is deserved."

In the justification of the ungodly, justice is seen, when God remits sins on account of love, though He Himself has mercifully infused that love. So we read of Magdalen: 'Many sins are forgiven her, because she hath loved much' (Luke 7:47)."

We may now move on to the discussion of matters in which both intellect and will are involved (qq. 22 to 24). This principally concerns what in us is the virtue of prudence, which in God is called Providence. This brings out the close connection between intellect and will and reason and choice (free will/freedom).

For the principal act of prudence is command, not judgment. This applies to the whole order of law, which in human affairs is the natural (moral) law beginning with synderesis – "seek good and shun evil" - and ending with the act of conscience, which applies the law to the situation, which is a judgment – "you ought to do this good or do not this evil". The need for prudence lies in the fact that actions are in the contingent and laws are in the universal. It carries out the original command of the first principle of the natural law, synderesis. This most universal command is carried through the first principles of the natural law, such as in regard to external goods to use them according to their universal destination of the good of all and each human individual person, then through natural institutions such as the institution of property, which has been distributed by the government on behalf of the whole community according to distributive justice and through positive laws of a general kind, such as the particular communities legislation regarding the rights of property and finally in the political prudence, principally had by the elected representatives of the people.

Sometimes St. Thomas will say that command is in the will, but when addressing the matter directly he says it is in the reason, with an act of will presupposed. For law is primarily to do with order (from extrinsic formal cause) whereas will brings in will-power (intelligent efficient cause). The word prudence is apparently a contraction of providence from Latin *pro-videre* to look ahead as the principal element of the moral habit. Being concerned with complex contingent matters it includes, of course, also hindsight, insight and circumspection.

It is significant that prudence is also associated in pre-modern times with sagacity or practical wisdom (a meaning kept in modern dictionaries). The modern notion of the key concept of prudence has, however, been eviscerated to mean a cautious opting out of difficult situations – a notion of caution that is not easy to distinguish from cowardice (witness the withdrawal from Afghanistan) - precisely because the champions of modern science have not only lost any real sense of wisdom but have vehemently rejected it, with the contempt for theoretical wisdom as the science of Metaphysics, from which has inevitably flowed the abandonment of practical wisdom in the science and "art" of Ethics, both general or personal and special or social. Within the latter come the new experimental, amoral, modern "sciences" of Politics and "Economics" (formerly called Political Economy). It is no coincidence that modern education is an education founded on folly.

St. Thomas explains how this notion of prudence is applied to divine providence: "it is necessary that the type of the order of things towards their end should pre-exist in the divine mind: and the type of things ordered towards an end is, properly speaking, providence. For it is the chief part of prudence, to which two other parts are directed—namely, remembrance of the past, and understanding of the present; inasmuch as from the remembrance of what is past and the understanding of what is present, we gather how to provide for the future. Now it belongs to prudence, according to the Philosopher (Ethic. vi, 12), to direct other things towards an end whether in regard to oneself—as for instance, a man is said to be prudent, who orders well his acts towards the end of life—or in regard to others subject to him, in a family, city or kingdom; in which sense it is said (Matthew 24:45), 'a faithful and wise servant, whom his lord hath appointed over his family.' In this way prudence or providence may suitably be attributed to God. For in God Himself there can be nothing ordered towards an end, since He is the last end. This type of order in things towards an end is therefore in God called providence. Whence Boethius says (De Consol. iv, 6) that 'Providence is the divine type itself, seated in the Supreme Ruler; which disposeth all things': which disposition may refer either to the type of the order of things towards an end, or to the type of the order of parts in the whole."

St. Thomas elaborates on this in his reply to objection 3: "Providence resides in the intellect; but presupposes the act of willing the end. Nobody gives a precept about things done for an end; unless he will that end. Hence prudence presupposes the moral virtues, by means of which the appetitive faculty is directed towards good, as the Philosopher says. Even if Providence has to do with the divine will and intellect equally, this would not affect the divine simplicity, since in God both the will and intellect are one and the same thing, as we have said above (Article 19)."

Then in article 4 he explains how divine providence governs things both necessary and contingent: "Divine providence imposes necessity upon some things; not upon all, as some formerly believed. For to providence it belongs to order things towards an end. Now after the divine goodness, which is an extrinsic end to all things, the principal good in things themselves is the perfection of the universe; which would not be, were not all grades of being found in things. Whence it pertains to divine providence to produce every grade of being. And thus it has prepared for some things necessary causes, so that they happen of necessity; for others contingent causes, that they may happen by contingency, according to the nature of their proximate causes."

We then move on from q. 22 to qq. 23 &24 which deal with predestination and the book of life. However St. Thomas's discussion of these two questions is complicated by the fact that the true end of human happiness is supernatural (Beatific Vision). This is a matter that has been the subject of much controversy in recent times (since de Lubac). From what St. Thomas has said in various places some have argued that such supernatural happiness is somehow "natural" in being naturally desired. The question is what would have been the nature of human happiness if God had not raised human nature to the supernatural level of grace, which has to be understood as an entirely gratuitous act on the part of God.

We do not wish to enter into this controversy here, though our position has been explained elsewhere in great detail. We will say a little about it however when we come to the last question 26 of this treatise on God as able to be understood from reason in Natural Theology.

Here we might only quote what St. Thomas says in article 8 of question 23 where he throws some light on the problem of divine predestination and human free will: "Wherefore we must say otherwise that in predestination two things are to be considered— namely, the divine ordination; and its effect. As regards the former, in no possible way can predestination be furthered by the prayers of the saints. For it is not due to their prayers that anyone is predestined by God. As regards the latter, predestination is said to be helped by the prayers of the saints, and by other good works; because providence , of which predestination is a part, does not do away with secondary causes but so provides effects, that the order of secondary causes falls also under providence. So, as natural effects are provided by God in such a way that Natural causes are directed to bring about those natural effects, without which those effects would not happen; so the salvation of a person is predestined by God in such a way, that whatever helps that person towards salvation falls under the order of predestination; whether it be one's own prayers or those of another; or other good works, and such like, without which one would not attain to salvation. Whence, the predestined must strive after good works and prayer; because through these means predestination is most certainly fulfilled. For this reason it is said: 'Labor more that by good works you may make sure your calling and election' (2 Peter 1:10)."

St. Augustine has apparently another way of explaining the relation between human free will and God's will. We have to thank God for all the good that we do even to the attainment of eternal happiness, but to blame ourselves for all the evil that comes to us even to our end being one of eternal misery. For without God our free will is not an efficient cause but a deficient one. So let us leave at that the problem of reconciling the certain existence of free will with the answers to questions 23 & 24.

The last question 26 returns to that of happiness as an attribute of God. But we need to consider first the question of power as an attribute of God in question 25. In our opinion, we should connect this with question 18, life as an attribute of God, the consideration of which we have postponed in order to do this. For as noted St. Thomas treats of God's power as something to be considered only in relation to creation.

The problem with this is that such a notion of power is consequential to the divine nature itself, and not intrinsic to God without any consideration of things other than God, as are all the other attributes dealt with. To deal with this we need to go into the notion of life, considered without reference to intellectual life, or knowledge, as something belonging to God.

When we look at the notion of life in this way in ourselves we note that we have vital functions that are not just in common with animals but also are in common with plants. To live is to be in a higher way than non-living existence, yet the higher level of existence of animals is by reason of knowledge, So too the higher level of spiritual existence, common to humans and angels, is by reason of intellectual knowledge. It is not that there is more than one life in these higher beings but their higher mode of actual being contains virtually all that is below them. So the human being for instance can be said to be (exist), to live (by unconscious life), to live by sense life (conscious life) and to live by intellectual life (the one soul being purely spiritual able to function at all three levels of life, but the lower two needing to be in and through a body.

So we find that we have vital power as well as cognitive and sense appetitive power and intellectual and will power. The general notion of power in a being of spiritual form cannot be separated from intellectual life but it can be considered abstracted from the bodily connection it necessarily has in living bodies.

Then when we come to consider power in God distinct from his intellect and will we can gain some insight into the infinite power and sheer vitality of the divine nature that follows from its pure act of being (*esse*). In terms of perfection of divine happiness we might be able to allow a notion of simple *joie de vivre* that accompanies the highest kind of life possible. Power as we see St. Thomas appropriate it to God signifies power flowing not from potency but from pure act. It is this notion of power that attaches to the act (*esse*) whereby the creature exists, lives and knows, especially at the highest level of spiritual life.

It is because of its enjoyment of *esse* as derived from God that the plant can be said to flourish (a term adopted in modern terms for human happiness). What is more this *joie de vivere* may be expressed at the animal and higher levels in the notion of play, that exulting in the very power and activity of one's existence. Some have even associated happiness with a kind of play that is had when one's work is done. It serves as rest but there is a higher meaning in the sense of a more perfect activity.

Thus we may get some insight into the association of Almighty with God even considered as one. Then in the consideration of the Trinity we see it appropriated to the Father as the first principle of the divine processions, which connected then with intellectual power, gives rise to the Father as the generative principle of the Son as Word. It is significant, however, that the notion of generation comes first from the level of life before that of intellect. Furthermore, Aristotle places generation as the distinction attribute of plant life, a more perfect demonstration of vital power than nutrition and growth.

It is the very nature of God then to generate his goodness which occurs within the very life of God supernaturally (but "naturally") and this is extended by an urge of generosity (good is self diffusive) that is nonetheless free and gratuitous in bringing into existence other beings according to some limited likeness of the divine nature, and elevating some of a spiritual nature, if having to be freely accepted, to an intimate participation in the enjoyment of the divine life itself.

So I speculate that the "property" attributed to the Father of being ungenerated (which is had in common with the Holy Spirit) is founded in the notion of life and power that pertains to the divinity before all other attributes. Thus with some hesitation in venturing into the exalted considerations of Sacred Theology I am emboldened to modify what St. Thomas has to say about power as an attribute of God that is taken through the relation of creation to God as Creator. I would suggest that this attribute may be explained without reference to creative power but simply to what belongs to the being (*esse*) and life (*vivere*) of God as pure act. Also this is something that can be explained within the limit of Natural Theology, or of God as one, according to the highest level of life, but not yet understood as triune.

We simply put here St. Thomas's response to the question in the first article of question 18 to bring out the different aspects of the notion of life: "We can gather to what things life belongs, and to what it does not, from such things as manifestly possess life. Now life manifestly belongs to animals, for it said in De Vegetab. i [De Plantis i, 1] that in animals life is manifest. We must, therefore, distinguish living from lifeless things, by comparing them to that by reason of which animals are said to live: and this it is in which life is manifested first and remains last. We say then that an animal begins to live when it begins to move of itself: and as long as such movement appears in it, so long as it is considered to be alive. When it no longer has any movement of itself, but is only moved by another power, then its life is said to fail, and the animal to be dead. Whereby it is clear that those things are properly called living that move themselves by some kind of movement, whether it be movement properly so called, as the act of an imperfect being, i.e. of a thing in potentiality, is called movement; or movement in a more general sense, as when said of the act of a perfect thing, as understanding and feeling are called movement. Accordingly all things are said to be alive that determine themselves to movement or operation of any kind: whereas those things that cannot by their nature do so, cannot be called living, unless by a similitude."

In article 2 St. Thomas draws attention to an important distinction in regard to the notion of life: "As is clear from what has been said (I:17:3), our intellect, which takes cognizance of the essence of a thing as its proper object, gains knowledge from sense, of which the proper objects are external accidents. Hence from external appearances we come to the knowledge of the essence of things. And because we name a thing in accordance with our knowledge of it, as is clear from what has already been said (I:13:1), so from external properties names are often imposed to signify essences. Hence such names are sometimes taken strictly to denote the essence itself, the signification of which is their principal object; but sometimes, and less strictly, to denote the properties by reason of which they are imposed. And so we see that the word 'body' is used to denote a genus of substances from the fact of their possessing three dimensions: and is sometimes taken to denote the dimensions themselves; in which sense body is said to be a species of quantity. The same must be said of life. The name is given from a certain external appearance, namely, self-movement, yet not precisely to signify this, but rather a substance to which self-movement and the application of itself to any kind of operation, belong naturally. To live, accordingly, is nothing else than to exist in this or that nature; and life signifies this, though in the abstract, just as the word 'running' denotes 'to run' in the abstract.

Hence 'living' is not an accidental but an essential predicate. Sometimes, however, life is used less properly for the operations from which its name is taken, and thus the Philosopher says (Ethic. ix, 9) that to live is principally to sense or to understand."

Then in article 3 St. Thomas shows how the notion of life applies to God: "Life is in the highest degree properly in God. In proof of which it must be considered that since a thing is said to live in so far as it operates of itself and not as moved by another, the more perfectly this power is found in anything, the more perfect is the life of that thing. In things that move and are moved, a threefold order is found. In the first place, the end moves the agent: and the principal agent is that which acts through its form, and sometimes it does so through some instrument that acts by virtue not of its own form, but of the principal agent, and does no more than execute the action. Accordingly there are things that move themselves, not in respect of any form or end naturally inherent in them, but only in respect of the executing of the movement; the form by which they act, and the end of the action being alike determined for them by their nature. Of this kind are plants, which move themselves according to their inherent nature, with regard only to executing the movements of growth and decay.

Other things have self-movement in a higher degree, that is, not only with regard to executing the movement, but even as regards to the form, the principle of movement, which form they acquire of themselves. Of this kind are animals, in which the principle of movement is not a naturally implanted form; but one received through sense. Hence the more perfect is their sense, the more perfect is their power of self-movement. Such as have only the sense of touch, as shellfish, move only with the motion of expansion and contraction; and thus their movement hardly exceeds that of plants. Whereas such as have the sensitive power in perfection, so as to recognize not only connection and touch, but also objects apart from themselves, can move themselves to a distance by progressive movement. Yet although animals of the latter kind receive through sense the form that is the principle of their movement, nevertheless they cannot of themselves propose to themselves the end of their operation, or movement; for this has been implanted in them by nature; and by natural instinct they are moved to any action through the form apprehended by sense. Hence such animals as move themselves in respect to an end they themselves propose are superior to these. This can only be done by reason and intellect; whose province it is to know the proportion between the end and the means to that end, and duly coordinate them. Hence a more perfect degree of life is that of intelligible beings; for their power of self-movement is more perfect. This is shown by the fact that in one and the same man the intellectual faculty moves the sensitive powers; and these by their command move the organs of movement. Thus in the arts we see that the art of using a ship, i.e. the art of navigation, rules the art of ship-designing; and this in its turn rules the art that is only concerned with preparing the material for the ship.

But although our intellect moves itself to some things, yet others are supplied by nature, as are first principles, which it cannot doubt; and the last end, which it cannot but will. Hence, although with respect to some things it moves itself, yet with regard to other things it must be moved by another. Wherefore that being whose act of understanding is its very nature, and which, in what it naturally possesses, is not determined by another, must have life in the most perfect degree. Such is God; and hence in Him principally is life. From this the Philosopher concludes (Metaph. xii, 51), after showing God to be intelligent, that God has life most perfect and eternal, since His intellect is most perfect and always in act."

Coming to the question of power (q. 25) we set out below what St. Thomas says in his response for Article 1 and answer to the first objection, in which it is clear that he is thinking of power not perhaps as completely relative to an extrinsic effect, but nonetheless tending to be explained in such a way. "Power is twofold—namely, passive, which exists not at all in God; and active, which we must assign to Him in the highest degree. For it is manifest that everything, according as it is in act and is perfect, is the active principle of something: whereas everything is passive according as it is deficient and imperfect. Now it was shown above (I:3:2; I:4:1 and I:4:2), that God is pure act, simply and in all ways perfect, nor in Him does any imperfection find place. Whence it most fittingly belongs to Him to be an active principle, and in no way whatsoever to be passive. On the other hand, the notion of active principle is consistent with active power. For active power is the principle of acting upon something else; whereas passive power is the principle of being acted upon by something else, as the Philosopher says (Metaph. v, 17). It remains, therefore, that in God there is active power in the highest degree."

"Reply to Objection 3. In creatures, power is the principle not only of action, but likewise of effect. Thus in God the idea of power is retained, inasmuch as it is the principle of an effect; not, however, as it is a principle of action, for this is the divine essence itself; except, perchance, after our manner of understanding, inasmuch as the divine essence, which pre-contains in itself all perfection that exists in created things, can be understood either under the notion of action, or under that of power; as also it is understood under the notion of 'suppositum' possessing nature, and under that of nature. Accordingly the notion of power is retained in God in so far as it is the principle of an effect." St. Thomas has noted that there is not one notion, as of substance and act, which are really distinct in creatures, wherein or whereby we can adequately represent the divine being, but that we have to use two or more to bring out different aspects of the one God. I leave it to the reader to judge whether my comments on this result in any modification of what St. Thomas says.

But we move on now to the final question prior to the treatment of the Trinity the question of happiness as an attribute of the divine nature. It is noteworthy that St. Thomas comments at the end: "We have now spoken enough concerning what pertains to the unity of the divine essence." As noted above there remains a problem with distinguishing natural happiness from supernatural happiness which is something that he does not address here. On the face of what he says at the end it would seem that he is not speaking about the beatific vision. However this is not all that clear.

Even so there is no problem with the question in the first article: Whether happiness (beatitude) belongs to God? It is in regard to the second article that some see a problem – of placing such happiness essentially in the act of intellect alone. It may be gathered from what we said above that we could see happiness as the perfect state of divine nature according to its three attributes, power, intellect and will. But it is in regard to the last two that argument persists. Can the act of will, which is finally joy in the rest that follows the desire for good, be excluded from the essence of happiness?

St. Thomas does address this in his reply to objection 2: "Since beatitude is a good, it is the object of the will; now the object is understood as prior to the act of a power. Whence in our manner of understanding, divine beatitude precedes the act of the will at rest in it. This cannot be other than the act of the intellect; and thus beatitude is to be found in an act of the intellect." He does address the same issue elsewhere where he makes the joy of resting in the ultimate good or end to follow necessarily from the vision of God "face to face".

We may see how in us each of the attributes of life, intellect and will follow a certain order. But in the end they coalesce in being but three aspects of the one happiness. Is it not said "Taste and see that the Lord is good?" This we may see at the sense level where knowledge and inclination are virtually the same in the basic sense of touch. More so must it be in God. Though vision is the best mode of knowledge in respect of the form had, touch is the most perfect mode in terms of union. Indeed, the same word infinitive "to feel" is used for both the act of cognition and affection/appetition at their most fundamental level.

Concluding Comments

We have addressed this subject matter as a special aspect of Metaphysics according to St. Thomas's treatment in the First Part of the *Summa Theologiae*. This has certain advantages not the least being that although the questions are philosophical they can be considered with the assistance of the light of Faith.

Another advantage is that the treatment can be most economical leaving out much of the discussion of objections that would be considered in a more purely philosophical discussion. A treatment of the subject as conducted by Aristotle in the last books of his Metaphysics would make for a much lengthier book. This we may see from a mere glance at St. Thomas's commentary on Aristotle's Metaphysics. Nonetheless the essence or gist of what can be found in Aristotle's Metaphysics is covered by what we have done.

We might take a short look, however, at how the subject of Natural Theology was treated in the *Metaphysics*. We have already noted that there are three aspects to the study of the subject of Metaphysics as a whole, which we have named Ontology, Epistemology and Natural Theology. Not knowing the intent of supernatural theology (called Sacred Theology to distinguish it from Natural Theology) Aristotle referred to his aspect of the study of Metaphysics as simply Theology. He also referred to Metaphysics as a whole as the divine science.

If we look closely at the structure of the Metaphysics we can roughly divide the (14) books into three parts, with Books 1– 4 allocated principally to Epistemology, books 5 –10 to Ontology and books 11-14 to Natural Theology. The last two books it will be noted St. Thomas elected not to comment upon, apparently because Aristotle had expounded what he regarded as the truth of the matter in books 11 &12 and these later books 13 & 14 were concerned with positions that he refuted. They do contain matters, however, that we will find useful to discuss in the context of the way modern science has developed. So we will say something about them in our next book, on Epistemology.

The philosophical treatment of Natural Theology could have been done by an examination of Books 11 & 12. However, there is much in Aristotle's treatment, even with the commentary of Aquinas, that is beholden to the multifarious details of the physics of the ancient world. This has caused much confused analysis by modern Aristotelian and even Thomist scholars apart from going into a lot of superfluous and antiquated theory. Not many make the effort to extract the basic principles and proofs upon which the final conclusions of Aristotle depend.

Book 11 is really but a summary of what Aristotle has laid down in the books leading up to his "theology" and we will not go over its contents. Aristotle is interested at this juncture in pointing out that the study of Metaphysics is primarily one of the study of substance and the task is to prove the kind of substance that God has to be, one, eternal and pure act. This is the core of Book 12.

There is much "undergrowth", however, in the nature of ancient concepts with regard to the nature of eternity allied with substance, e g. the view of the heavens, that needs to be cleared away. Aristotle thought of Metaphysics as the study of substance, which he described as "separate", meaning thereby separate totally from matter.

But he comes to this after considering substance as divisible into three, two of which belonged to the physical world of motion and the third to the metaphysical. He engages on a rather convoluted argument to the substance that is God.

He divided the physical universe into two parts according to two notions of matter. The one is the order of material things with which we are most familiar, subject to generation and corruption according to substantial change. For the other he tended to adopt the ancient notion of the heavens being made up of bodies, but incorruptible and subject to only one kind of change (or motion), circular local motion. This bodily order he referred to as "eternal".

In modern times we have to drop this distinction between bodies – there is now no sense in attributing anything eternal, by way of motion or time, to sensible things of any kind. Thus we have to abstract from all that Aristotle (and even Aquinas) says about this view of the physical universe. Curiously, though it is rather incongruous in the overall picture, Aristotle did allow for pure spirits as somehow "prime movers" in this order of celestial bodies.

The notion of eternity therefore gets quite ingeniously complicated. St. Thomas will elsewhere put the duration applicable to angels as not of time strictly taken but of *aevum*, which again is not strictly eternity. Eternity belongs properly only to God. So we have a deal of sifting to do in bringing out the essential thrust of Aristotle's argument. In the context of all the other material considered this is not easy even with St. Thomas's help.

Many get mixed up with Aristotle's proof of God as the first unmoved mover in the Physics, which he refers to in the Metaphysics.

But, what is not noticed is what St. Thomas says about this way in nn.2497 & 2498 in Book 12.

"2497. Yet it should be noted that the arguments which he introduces in Book VIII of the *Physics*, which he assumes as the basis of his procedure here, are not demonstrations in the strict sense but only dialectical arguments; unless perhaps they are arguments against the positions of the ancient natural philosophers regarding the beginning of motion, inasmuch as he aims to destroy these positions.

2498. And aside from the other arguments which he does not touch upon here, it is evident that the argument which he does give here to prove that time is eternal is not demonstrative. For if we suppose that at some moment time began to be, it is not necessary to assume a prior moment except in imaginary time; just as when we say that there is no body outside of the heavens what we mean by "outside" is merely an imaginary something. Hence, just as it is not necessary to posit some place outside of the heavens, even though "outside" seems to signify place, so too neither is it necessary that there be a time before time began to be or a time after time will cease to be, even though before and after signify time."

So St. Thomas says that such an "eternity" of time cannot be proved from reason. But that does not mean a beginning in time can be. The beginning is entirely within the freedom of the divine will. We may only note the distinction between God's absolute and ordinate will.

No doubt the influence of Mathematics upon imaginations, ancient and modern, mislead many here; they appear not able to distinguish from a notion of time that is real and one that is imaginary.

Incidentally, another misconception that is prevalent is the belief that Metaphysics is not concerned with objects that are sensible. This is what St. Thomas says in n. 2427: "Hence this science (first philosophy) considers both sensible substances and immovable substances inasmuch as both are beings and substances." Even among respected modern Thomists we have a distinction made between modern experimental science and natural science or philosophy as understood by Aquinas in that the object of the former is mobile being as mobile and of the latter is mobile being as being, the latter clearly a metaphysical consideration.

However, we should say something here about the difference between Physics and Mathematics as understood by Aristotle and Aquinas. We will deal with it more fully in our last book in this series, *Natural Philosophy, Modern Science and Saint Thomas Aquinas*. The object of Mathematics and accordingly its distinction both from Physics and Metaphysics has proved to be a problem from the beginning of the discussion of philosophy and science. We can see this as far back as Pythagoras and it remained an unresolved problem in Plato. It is resolved to some extent by Aristotle but there are aspects of its treatment that are still problematic even in Aquinas. The notion of "intelligible matter" for instance is something that needs much deeper analysis.

It should be insisted upon that the objects of Mathematics are abstracted from matter to a greater degree than those of Physics or Natural Science. Nonetheless, this abstraction is not totally from matter. Aquinas tries to get around the problem by distinguishing between the condition of the object relative to *esse* or real existence and according to what he refers to *ratio* or "reason" (awkwardly

translated as "structural form"). To our mind this is not entirely satisfactory. But we must leave the critique of this notion to our book
on Mathematics, where we need to look at also the modern treatment of the science not only in its pure state but also in its mixed
state called mathematical physics.

Here we are concerned only to consider Aristotle's proof for the
existence of God in Book 12 of his Metaphysics. The proof seems to
depend upon time and motion being eternal. For Aristotle relies on
this to posit the need for the cause of things of our experience to be
eternal. But as we have seen St. Thomas has said that we cannot
prove apodictically that the temporal world is eternal and the proofs
given by Aristotle are dialectical which means arguments that may
be effective against another but not in themselves demonstrative.
(see nn. 2497 & 2498 above quoted)

However, St. Thomas says that despite this "the things which are
proved about the eternity and immateriality of the first substance
necessarily follow". This he explains in n. 2499. "But even if the arguments which prove that motion and time are eternal are not
demonstrative and necessarily conclusive, still the things which are
proved about the eternity and immateriality of the first substance
necessarily follow; for, even if the world were not eternal, it would
still have to be brought into being by something that has prior existence. And if this cause were not eternal, it too would have to be
produced by something else. But since there cannot be an infinite
series, as has been proved in Book II (153: C 301-4), it is necessary
to posit an eternal substance whose essence contains no potentiality
and is therefore immaterial."

Because whatever is regarded as constituted as having potency in any way, if it exists, "in being" signifying that it has existence, it cannot have given itself that "being" (esse) for by its nature or essence it has only potential for this actual state. The proof comes not from the length of time that the creature is contingent but from the very nature of its essence expressing a potential only "to be". Bringing in the conditions of motion and time that apply to material beings only clouds the notion of the relevant contingency with which we are concerned.

The forms or essences of purely spiritual beings, "separate" from matter, exist also contingently, because their essence names a mere potential to be. All contingent existence is a received existence from one who "owns" it, which is God, as pure act of esse. Once we understand the basic division of being (ens) which we have from creatures into potency and act the proof follows quite simply. So too do all the other "properties" of the Creator or God as One dealt with by St. Thomas in the beginning of his Summa, God's absolute simplicity, etc.

Then with some help from Faith in the nature of God as Trinity, we can see how the five ways elaborated by St. Thomas can be related to the five causes, three extrinsic, efficient, exemplary and final, and two intrinsic, formal and material. God as pure act has a three-fold causality, almighty power appropriated to the Father, the eternal principle of the Son, to whom is appropriated the Wisdom according to which things are created and the final causality that from our point of view moves both Father and Son as joint eternal principle of the Holy Spirit, to whom is appropriated the Love that that inspires all divine activity. Of course, only a person of Faith can make this connection.

But a reflection of this may be seen in the work of a human artist. The builder is the principal efficient cause, the architect provides the idea as the exemplar, and the desire for a home in a couple motivates the whole process. The material cause is evident in the materials needed in which the form is to be put. It is only the purely formal cause that is missing if we do not know the order of spiritual creation.

What has happened in the modern era is a peculiar ignoring of the need for an efficient cause other than ourselves. Things spring wondrously, as in the case of Descartes, out of our own minds. The "world" of the modern mind even of the scientist is spent almost exclusively in imagination. The mad scientist lives in the plan room conversing with those who would give him the money that motivates his whole project. He never gets round to doing anything.

So it is that with regard to our understanding of nature and reality the existence of the Creator is dispensed with. Pope Benedict XVI has explained how this has affected even the study of Modern Theology. We have a bit more to say on this in Appendix A. But, on the other hand, more generally we can see how this neglect of the Almighty as Creator has impacted on all modern human Philosophy. Metaphysics as Natural Theology has entirely disappeared from modern science. We explore the implications of this a bit more in Appendix B.

Virtually the only hope for a return to reality and sanity is a restoration of the study of Thomas of the Creator.

Appendices

The two appendices we add are meant to place some light on the two errors to which the modern mind, including that of some Catholic theologians, are drawn in regard to the question considered in this book, namely, that of the proper position to take in regard to creation and generally the relation between the orders of Faith and Reason. These two errors are those referred to in Pope Saint Paul VI's Lumen ecclesiae, which he named Naturalism and Supernaturalism (quoted in our book "Thomist Tradition: Avoiding Scylla and Charybdis"). Alternatively, they may be called Fideism and Rationalism. The latter wants us to appeal solely to human reason to the exclusion of divine Faith whilst the former to divine Faith to the exclusion of human reason. Both errors not only mistake the relation between Faith and Reason but also distort the proper notions of (Christian) Grace and (Human) Nature. The modern presentations of these errors have certain peculiarities, which we hope to bring out in the appendices.

For instance, the error of Naturalism is taken to a more extreme position that not only rejects the theological value of Faith but also the philosophical value of Metaphysics. This makes such an error such a distortion of the notion of science that it may be termed Scientism. This we deal with the first appendix.

On the other hand, the modern version of the error of Supernaturalism reacts so vehemently against this extreme version of Naturalism that it resorts to a virtual erasing altogether the idea of nature as distinct from grace applying to human beings in their actual condition of being created as ordered to supernatural happiness. This we deal with in the second appendix. It may be appreciated that the problems having to be addressed are quite complicated and it is not surprising that they have given rise to much controversy. We may however locate the root cause of both errors in their modern versions in a rejection of or weakness in Metaphysics that results in having a distorted notion of nature.

We therefore treat first of the error of Naturalism in its modern dress under the title of "God and the Theory of Everything" and second of Supernaturalism in the form of a critique of a defence of the well discussed position of Henri de Lubac by Nicholas J Healy III.

Appendix A

God and the Theory of Everything

For Aristotle the endeavour to discover the theory of everything necessarily belongs not to Physics but to Metaphysics. The philosophers of the modern era (whose way of thinking modern scientists have generally gone along with) have come to reject the notion that Metaphysics, as understood by Aristotle, has any cognitive value. What this has meant is that the explanations of everything (reduced now to "phenomena" and "events") are sought entirely within the world of material reality or what is available to sense observation and verification.

Of recent times physicists have begun to talk in terms of being on the verge of discovering the ultimate explanation of physical reality, of constructing a "theory of everything". We do not pretend to have any great insight into the particular details of what these scientists are referring to. As in most matters of science today the general public, and indeed philosophers of considerable standing, do not have the necessary experience in regard to the experiments conducted, or sufficient mathematical expertise in regard to the esoteric concepts dealt with, to know what exactly is intended by the theories and formulas discussed. So it is very much a matter of (human) faith for all but a select few of us. Not that that is a bad thing; on the whole such faith is quite evidently well founded under modern conditions of communication between scientists.

All that we need is an "educated" awareness of what is being talked about so as to test the conclusions and theories against logic and common sense. Nor do we need to be put off by the sometimes strange names given to objects reasoned to and the seemingly contradictory propositions put forward in an effort to explain new phenomena so concluded to by the scientists. For, as Aristotle himself pointed out, in the order of physical reality there is much evidence of opposition in nature and in a thing's properties and relations. There cannot be any true contradiction in things but the use of the language of contradiction generally stems from a lack of grounding in Aristotelian logic, and a failure to note the difference between contradictory and contrary opposition.

There is then a great deal of "interpretation" involved in determining what exactly is intended in the language of modern physics. Especially is this so since the development of the New Physics. But we can make some general observations. If the previous absolutist Newtonian physics erred by placing too much faith in a totally deterministic vision of the material universe the new relativistic physics runs the risk of veering to the other extreme of pure indeterminism. Some celebrated physicist/mathematicians whose minds turn to philosophise upon the current state of their science then indulge in a language of absurdity that would outdo if possible the "dialectic" of a Hegelian.

But we do not wish to deny the genuine insights of scientists as a whole. Moreover, they are entitled to use whatever language is useful for their purposes, provided they do not go beyond the limits of their particular fields of enquiry.

The esoteric concepts and propositions that have been developed in modern mathematical physics have generated an array of names and descriptions that boggle the imagination. Built upon a description of the fundamental forces of nature which have been reduced to four, gravitation, electromagnetism, and the strong and weak nuclear forces, we have, not to mention the more familiar protons, neutrons and electrons, names such as quarks, subdivided into up and down, strange and charm, top and bottom. These are held together by the strong force referred to, mediated by gluons. Electromagnetic forces, it seems, are mediated by exchange of photons. Hadrons are composites of quarks.

A hyperon is described as any baryon containing one or more strange quarks, but no charm quarks or bottom quarks. A baryon is a composite subatomic particle made up of three quarks (as distinct from mesons, which comprise one quark and one antiquark). And so the nomenclature develops as more and more particles are discovered. However, bosons and fermions deserve special mention as they are regarded as constituting the two basic kinds of things or forces within the universe. Of late, attention is focused upon the Higgs boson, now almost a household name, which it is believed will go towards explaining the origin of mass.

But it is not necessary for the purposes of this article to delve into the details of these scientific concepts and theories. For our argument is that modern science, or more specifically mathematical physics is not so constituted as to be able to provide a truly ultimate explanation of anything, let alone a theory of everything. Genuine scientists, such as Higgs, are quite conscious of this and are embarrassed to find their scientific work referred to in such terms, popularised now in the phrase "the God particle", which, if used by Higgs himself, was so only in jest.

Not that the modern scientist is not striving to know more and more about physical reality, and in that sense seeking to arrive at an ultimate explanation, but he is doing so only according to the limitations of his lines of investigation. It is the purpose of this article to examine what these limitations are and show that, though the more universal language of metaphysics is used by physicists, it is only taken literally by those modern philosophers of science (and admittedly by many celebrated physicists who go along with their thinking) who are basically materialists, but of the more sophisticated kind common today, i.e. those who mix up mathematics with metaphysics (meta-physics as explained below) and believe that everything can be explained universally and ultimately in what are in fact particularist and materialistic (mechanistic) terms.

The modern view is not a crudely empiricist position. For it allows for the contribution of Mathematics towards our understanding of empirical reality. Indeed, if anything, the objects of Mathematics dominate the picture of reality as conceived in modern science so that it is not simply what is sensibly observable which is determinative for the scientific method but what is also conceivable according to the creative ability of the human imagination.

This introduces a complication and indeed a kind of opposition into the modern concept of (material) reality. We might put it that in the modern concept of science Mathematics plays the role of a meta-physics, not in the Aristotelian sense, but as relating to a strange order or "dimension" of reality, as we can know it, that transcends the purely empirical.

It is rather reminiscent of Plato's treatment of mathematical objects. For he accorded to them a reality that was distinct from the material order of things, and placed them more with the spiritual or metaphysical (in the Aristotelian sense) than with the material or physical. The modern mind, however, seems to place them at a level of reality that is below the metaphysical yet above the physical in their original Aristotelian senses.

An Aristotelian would say that the problem can only be properly resolved by distinguishing the twofold division of things (into material and spiritual) in the real from their threefold division (into physical, mathematical and metaphysical) in the mind by abstraction. The reality to which mathematically abstract objects relate remains within the physical or material order. The instinct of the modern mind then to disconnect them from the spiritual and metaphysical is surer than that of Plato.

The nature of the connection of mathematical objects with the physical or empirical world, however, remains puzzling, leading to all sorts of conundrums and queer interpretations of "reality". It is quite confidently believed that the imaginative objects worked upon by the mathematician, or rather mathematical physicist, is the key area in which to look for ultimate explanations in science. Yet, there is no denying the subordination of the formal treatment of mathematics to the empiricist/materialist basis of modern science.

This double orientation would be difficult to understand if all sciences had to be understood in simple terms (as in pure empirical science, pure mathematics etc.). But the duplex character of the object of a science is readily understandable if we are dealing with what was called by Aristotelians and Thomists a mixed or medial science (which modern science in our view comes closest to being). It is a basic fault then with the modern philosophy of science to attempt to think of this notion of science and the scientific method in simplistic terms, like the ancient atomists.

Astronomy is the classical example given by the ancients and mediaevals of a mixed or physico-mathematical science. And we might say that nuclear physics is modeled on such a physio-mathematical investigation of the basic elements of physical reality. Indeed, right from Galileo and Newton we have had the intimate association of modern physical science with mathematics, where the secrets of nature are thought to be best revealed by recourse to mathematical principles and methods.

Considering generally the nature of such mixed sciences St. Thomas asked the question whether they are more mathematical or physical. The answer given is that they are formally mathematical but materially physical. That makes mathematics the higher level of scientific analysis in such a science. But that does not finally settle the question in favour of mathematics. For the form with which mathematics is concerned is something accidental (quantity), whilst the "matter" which physics investigates, despite being by means of sensible accidents (such as qualities, motion etc.), is something substantial (nature understood as bodily reality).

St. Thomas put it that it is the physical objects, though the material part of the science, which the science is ultimately aiming to understand. On this more fundamental score, then, the science is more physical than mathematical. This is evident in that the conclusions arrived at in the science by mathematical methods need to be verified by physical observation or empirical means. It is not good for the science when the modern physicist lets his mathematical imagination run away with him (as is often the case, as, for instance, with Stephen Hawking).

This explanation by St. Thomas cannot be understood by the modern mind, for it has ruled out in principle or *a priori* the proper notion of substance as applied to physical reality. Yet, this analysis is verified in the attempts by the modern scientists, as "physicists", to discover the ultimate explanation in science (Mathematical Physics being science in the purest sense in modern thinking). For though the investigations are dominated by mathematical explanations (of a formal kind) the general thrust of the investigations is towards discovering the ultimate "particle" or "force" as understood in physical or empirical terms. In the end therefore the investigation is ordered to a definite vision of the nature of observable or physical reality interpreted in purely material terms.

So it is that the mathematical analysis goes along with the general reductive tendency in explanations in terms of purely material causality. Like a child trying to know what makes something (e. g. a clock) "tick", the modern (mathematical) physicist takes things apart and, not satisfied with natural means of division or partition of the physical bodies, moves on to employ sophisticated instrumental and even violent means (all quite legitimate in the cause of science). He has succeeded in splitting the atom (the unsplittable in ancient theory). The more elementary parts ("particles") thereby discovered have proved able to be further divided with the application of greater force.

Fundamentally, then, despite the prominence of the work of the imagination and mathematical abstraction in the modern scientific endeavour, the line of explanation follows what Aristotle identified as that of material causality. The search for an ultimate explanation, or "theory of everything", is a search for the ultimate material element or "particle", if one is thinking in (more static) terms of substance or being, or for the ultimate "event", if one is thinking in (more dynamic) terms of energy or function (expressed in some formula or other).

We should note, however, that the universalist language used by modern physicists does not have the universality it ordinarily has. It can be used in relation to a quite specialised area of scientific endeavour but then it has to be clearly understood as strictly qualified and limited. Before pursuing the limitations needed to be imposed upon the move to an ultimate explanation of reality modern science is taking us let us endeavour to understand in Aristotelian terms, then, how it seems that modern mathematical physics is taken to be the most basic level of science and indeed how mathematical analysis seems to have taken on the dominant role in the ultimate understanding of physical reality.

It is highly significant that since Descartes, in regard to the question of which is the more substantial part of science, the relation has been inverted. For Descartes made quantity (extension) the substance of bodily reality. This has had the effect of confusing the relation between the objects of Physics and Mathematics, making it appear that the mixed science was a simple one. Mathematics, from being only the formal part of modern science, and that focused on an accident (of quantity), took on also the role of being the substantial part, thus usurping the role of physics considered (in classical natural philosophy) as an empirical science, i.e. as the science of physical substances or bodies.

In the history of modern philosophy this is highlighted by a curious consequence. As Locke noted, physical properties other than those stemming from quantity, such as the qualities of hardness, heat, colour etc, thereby lost their "objective" status, as really inhering in material substances, and were reduced to a "subjective" status, epiphenomena of our faculties of knowledge. Only quantitative properties of bodies, such as size, shape etc., were "primary qualities", by which was understood that they only enjoyed the substantial reality of quantity, independent of mind.

The effect of this disconnection of "secondary qualities" from the objective order grounded in substance, however, as Hume quickly noted, was to undermine the real basis of all human knowledge, ironically of science itself. Descartes' attempt to save our certainties from within the mind had ended in a skepticism more radical than any.

Ignoring this philosophical/metaphysical consequence, the modern mind happily consented to work with the combination of the mathematical method of Descartes and the empirical method of Locke, with quantity viewed somehow as the fundamental language of the structure of nature and "phenomena" as its materials. Necessarily this became equivalent to a mechanistic view of the material universe. Galileo's and Newton's science came to be a vision of systematic knowledge of observable phenomena in principle fully determinable according to mathematical laws or formulas. God was not excluded from this worldview, but he was to be viewed as the great Architect whose plan of creation could be read by us, or at least by expert mathematical physicists (called for short "Science").

The search for the ultimate explanations of things, as somehow a deeper insight into the workings of nature, necessarily stopped then at the level of quantity. But, in the mixed or medial science this notion of quantity is tied to the physical order, for it is a physico-mathematics, or mathematical physics, which is indulged in. Its object is not simply abstract quantity as dealt with in Mathematics proper, but concrete quantity, or the physical accident of quantity as found in bodily things, which indeed underlies all the other accidents, but is not to be equated with substance.

Physics and Mathematics are thus in some way fused, and accordingly imagination works in tandem with empirical experience ("observation and experiment"). Mathematics becomes an applied mathematics. Whereas in Mathematics proper there is no study of motion strictly taken now we see the use of vectors as well as scalar quantities. It is here that the modern physicist (delving ever more deeply into the inner reality of physical bodies) finds that order or structure of parts within the whole body at which he can only marvel.

Unbeknown to the modern physicist, however, it is not an order within the true bodily substance of such things which is being explored and expounded upon but an order of quantitative parts within a quantitative whole (a body seen in terms of dimensions or measurements only). Following out the modern line of thinking derived from the "metaphysics" of Descartes, the modern scientist is satisfied that that is all there is to the substance of material things.

This, incidentally, is the order in which we tend to talk of "design", or quantitative form (or formula), rather than substantial form.

In this view of things, the notion of a Creator God is demeaned to that of a Master Engineer or supremely intelligent Designer of a creation that is limited to something material only. (Hence, the paleness of Paley's proofs for the existence of God). The universe indeed comes to be conceived after the fashion of a giant machine, an artificial thing, and therefore not in principle beyond the "creative" reach of the human imagination and the "art" of man. Kant's objections to the proofs for the existence of God are based upon this mechanistic conception of nature.

What of substance the natural philosopher (or natural scientist in the classical language of Aristotle) can detect through a study of natural bodies' activities and properties has, for the reasons given, evaporated. The necessarily composite nature of bodies into purely intelligible formal and material principles means nothing. Moreover, by an inexorable process of reduction, the universe is reduced to a dead, lifeless machine-like entity, empty of higher forms, such as life and spirit.

That however is not to deny the marvelous and intricate order that is at the level of quantity. We are not concerned to deny that such a concept of the material universe has a beauty of its own that can stir the soul of the scientist. But, philosophically considered, it is a partial and lifeless image that misses completely the true grandeur of even the material order of things. Lost to the natural scientist, so dominated by Mathematics, is the sense of awe that we should have before the wonder and beauty of the natural world.

We should note at this point that the modern scientist is not primarily concerned with expounding the meaning of the world he investigates but with enabling the findings of science to be applied for the benefit of humanity. In further agreement with the original promoters of the modern scientific revolution, Rene Descartes and Francis Bacon, the aim of modern science is not so much to understand reality as to put such knowledge as it can gain to good use, for the benefit of humanity. The practical end takes over from the theoretical. Truth is tied to Utility: Science to Technology.

Accordingly, an ultimate theory of everything is not sought so much for its own sake but in the belief that thereby mankind may secure ultimate mastery of nature generally, and indeed of human nature itself. The search for the ultimate "theory of everything" remains a strong motivation, but it is not primary. Behind this is the belief that a good theoretical knowledge of science will be productive. Knowledge for its own sake is good. But better is knowledge that is power.

Let us return for the moment, however, to the theoretical side of science and the search for ultimate explanations in modern physics. We have noted above how Mathematics, from being only the formal part of modern science, and that focused on an accident (of quantity), took on also the role of being the substantial part, thus usurping the authority of physics or empirical science as the proper science of (material) "reality", or bodies. This inversion was helped by the objects of natural science, i.e. the non-quantitative qualities and actions of things, being taken merely as subjective, or "phenomena" only. Mathematics came to be the only "real" way to read nature, and the distinction between pure and applied Mathematics virtually disappeared.

Though now immersed in the material or concrete order of reality the formal character of the object and method of Mathematics nonetheless remains. Hence, the search for an ultimate explanation of reality along the lines of material causality acquires a strange formal and ideal character, and is often taken for a search for the ultimate mathematically conceived unit, like the "singularity" spoken of in the Big Bang Theory. Yet the elusive ultimate particle has to be at the same time something able to account for mass.

This insertion of the mathematical imagination into the search for the ultimate physical element (whether statically or dynamically conceived) gives a quite exotic character to this scientific effort. However, this does not alter the fact that the scientific endeavour here is of the nature of an attempt to find the ultimate explanation of reality by pursuing it as far as one can in the line of material causality. And it is here that the limitations necessarily applying to this scientific approach come to the fore.

For the revolution in science and scientific method that characterizes the modern age is not only in a rejection of Metaphysics as understood by Aristotle – this in fact came later – but also, and more radically so, in a rejection of his notion of science generally, with which went his doctrine of the four causes.

Various factors worked to bring down his philosophy of science, not the least was the discrediting of the Greek astronomy which he took over and incorporated into his general natural philosophy. Curiously enough, it was the applied mathematical side that collapsed. But this came about though better observational findings and meas-

urements. These showed that the physico-mathematical theories
constructed upon ancient data had been too speculative, even
though they were ingenious speculations which "saved the appearances" on the observational data available.

It was the empirical part of the ancient astronomy, therefore,
that was found to be source of the deficiency – and that largely because of the invention of new and better instruments of observation,
such as the telescope. The astronomical phenomena or appearances
were found not to be as they had been thought to be for centuries.
This led to the need for a major revision not just of astronomy but
also of natural science as a whole. One could say that the world was
turned upside down, a revolution in thinking that of itself would
have been profoundly unsettling for any society. That was the effect
of the revision of explanations in only one science. At the same time
scientific positions and theories of ancient lineage in all kinds of
fields were having to be revised as the spirit of empirical investigation of nature gathered momentum.

For it has to be said that during the earlier period of the Christian era relatively little attention was directed towards the empirical
study of nature for its own sake, and therefore to the development
the sciences of nature and the necessary correction of theories thus
found to be inadequate. This may be attributed to the greater focus
on the next life and the concentration on theology rather than philosophy. But it was also and significantly so because of the dominance of a platonic view of the bodily world, which found favour
with the early theologians. The tendency was then to present natural
things and events in a spiritualistic and symbolic way.

"Such denaturalization of the natural world", as Josef Pieper said, "sooner or later had to become intolerable; it is simply impossible to live a healthy and human life in a world populated exclusively by symbols" ("The Introduction to St. Thomas", p.47) The re-naturalization of the natural world is the defining feature of the modern era. It was a good thing in itself. As we shall argue, it was unfortunate that it was accompanied by a false philosophy of science which excluded the more important lines of explanation according to final and substantial formal causation and reduced the notion of science to the methods of a medial science which itself then combined a flawed understanding of material causation with a superficial understanding of formal causation (limited to the order of quantity only).

It need not have involved a rejection of religion but, as it turned out, it did. For though there was a genuine reason for rejecting not just an antiquated view of science but one that was holding back its progress, other extrinsic factors came into play. The most important, as is well known, was the spirit of rebellion against the Catholic Church. Here again there were legitimate grounds to call for reform. But it resulted in the wholesale rejection of the authority of the Church and her theology.

A similar thing happened to the "authority" of Aristotle and his philosophy. The flashpoint here was his natural philosophy, equated with natural science, and allied with what we have seen called medi-al science or mixed physical and mathematical science. Pure mathematical science was largely unaffected by the scientific "revolu-tion". As seen above, there were legitimate grounds for the reform of science as largely identified with Aristotle at the time. But the reaction was so strong that he was thrown out "lock, stock and bar-rel".

That this was so is quite ironic. For Aristotle was a relative new-comer onto the scene so far as philosophy was concerned and among the Greeks, a race of geniuses, he was the champion of em-pirical investigation in the natural sciences. Indeed, we may go as far as to say that it was the re-discovery of him in the heart of the Middle Ages that gave a great impetus to the revival of the empirical sciences. If he shared in the tendency of Greek science to speculate too much upon a narrow empirical base, he embodied as much as any in the history of science even up to the present day the spirit of empirical investigation and experimentation. This can be seen in the mediaeval theologian who most took on the spirit of Aristotle in the study of nature, St. Albert the Great.

Moreover, Aristotle clearly identified the fault that is the major reason for the "conservatism" of science in every age, not excluding his own. He had the spirit of genuine scientific enquiry more than any other, but even he had to work with the state of knowledge of his time which, as it turned out, was filled out with much specula-tive thinking based upon insufficient evidence. Later investigations were to overthrow nearly all Greek theories of the nature of things astronomical and chemical, though much of that which came within the available range of experience, such as biology and zoology, in which respect Aristotle's scientific work was particularly experience based, withstood the test of time.

But Aristotle warned against being too "rational" in one's phi-losophy of nature. There is an almost irresistible temptation in man to extrapolate his theorizing beyond the available evidence. The modern mind is keenly aware of this but in its philosophy of science goes to the opposite extreme of regarding all general conclusions about things in nature as hypothetical only and incurably so. That attitude flows from and supports a philosophy of radical skepticism, which is plainly false and absurd. In attempting to counter the rationalistic trait in scientific thinking some, such as Kuhn, go too far the other (relativist) way.

Despite this "philosophical" position (or lack of one), however, the modern age is just as prone as were the ancients to re-construct the universe according to its own imagined version of things. Such tendency to rationalism is particularly present in mathematical men of genius, such as Descartes. There is a difference however between the rationalistic "conservatism" in ancient and modern thinking. The grand speculative theories of the Greeks lasted a thousand years; in the modern age they are much more short lived. But that can be explained by the fact that the empirical spirit became dormant with the break up of the ancient world and, curiously enough, largely by reason of the prominence of the influence of Plato over Aristotle.

With the revival of the empirical spirit in the late mediaeval and early modern period such extrapolated speculation as occurred was overtaken rapidly by new discoveries requiring the grand theories to be constantly revised. In more recent times the rate of change seems to have accelerated (prompting Kuhn's thesis). Newton's deterministic physics was overtaken by Einstein's relativistic physics, which in turn had to accommodate quantum mechanics, much to his chagrin. Now scientists have begun to refer to the "old' quantum theory.

But within the time frame in which the boldest speculations hold the stage scientific conservatism reigns stronger than ever. Who is bold enough to challenge today the ultimate truth of the Big Bang Theory, which is only the latest grand speculation built upon the evidence available? In all likelihood, given the dizzying advances made in experimental research, is it not possible that in a few short years we may all be paying homage to the Little Fizzle Theory? It is not so much a matter of holding that such theoretical speculation is false, or indeed useless, but that it only "saves the appearances", as St. Thomas explained about the Ptolemaic Astronomy, and that it does not exclude the possibility of another theory doing just as well or better.

But the advantage modern science has, in its practitioners if not in its theorists, lies in the return to realism and, if you like, a true materialism/empiricism in regard to the study of the natural world, including the bodily part of human nature. Our practical caution against materialism in regard to our moral life should not be allowed to affect our theoretical study of physical nature, nor indeed the physical side of our human nature. The Church by no means is against natural science, or for that matter modern astronomy and nuclear physics. Indeed, St. Thomas endorses the keen study of the natural material world as necessary to a proper understanding of God, its author.

Thus there is no conflict between religion and science, rather the opposite if the Church's position is properly understood. Of the philosophical positions held today that of the Church is the most supportive of reason and science. This applies especially with regard to the emphasis give in modern times to the empirical side of science. This is precisely the aspect of science that St. Thomas adopted in favouring Aristotle over Plato (and Augustine) in the interpretation of material and human nature, even to the extent of basing human knowledge squarely upon the senses, so much so as to go along with Aristotle's claim that one's degree of intelligence is proportioned to one's sensitivity at the level of touch. The union between the spiritual soul and the material body in man could not be conceived as more intimate.

The conflicts of the past which have been read as between religion and science are owing to a superficial, and often prejudicial, reading of history. As is clear from the above, it is conservative scientists who provide the greatest resistance to any great theoretical change, let alone of a revolutionary kind, in the grand theories of the time. The innovators too are not always without blame, accusing those who resist what are often radical changes in thinking of obscurantism. Einstein, as is well known, never fully accepted quantum theory and seems to have been accused by some as having wasted the later part of his life contending against it.

However, we are not primarily concerned in this essay to criticize the tendency to rationalism and conservatism in modern science. For it is not something peculiar to the modern era but, as noted, something common to every age of science. It is dealt with here to counter the suggestion that modern scientists are free of this fault, despite their professed commitment to science founded in observation, experience and experiment. It is not rationalism which distinguishes modern natural science from ancient natural philosophy, or the modern scientific method from the Aristotelian. It is, as we intend to show, the opposite error pointed out also by Aristotle, which is an inordinate leaning to a false materialism in the study of nature.

Aristotle identified the rationalistic fault in method in the course of discussing the correct approach to the investigation of physical nature or material reality. Those with any knowledge of his philosophy of nature will be aware that it is based on his doctrine of hylemorphism. That is to say, every actual body or material substance is constituted of two contrary principles, called substantial form (*morphe*) and primary matter (*hyle*). Hence, it is a mistake to attempt to explain the nature of any material thing by reference to one simple line of causality. No body or part of a body, however minute, is simple, but is essentially composite. No amount of scientific analysis will uncover a basic simple physical unit (contrary to what happens in pure mathematical analysis).

Hence, a purely material line of investigation or analysis will not produce an adequate science of nature. The attempt to do so (which we argue is the fundamental motivation behind modern science and scientific method) is what may be called "materialism" (for which "empiricism" is another more subjective name). It should be noted, however, that for Aristotle, the materialistic or empiricist mode of investigation in regard to physical nature is not so much false as incomplete. It is only if it is not completed by a proper consideration of the formal principle (and that in the order of substance, not quantity), and especially if this is explicitly rejected, that it becomes false. On the other hand, the purely formalistic, or rationalist, mode of proceeding in the consideration of the natural world is false *per se*. For one cannot deal with material reality without taking matter immediately into account.

The same applies in the order of knowledge. One cannot do physics without verifying one's scientific conclusions by reference to sense experience. In the science of nature empiricism is the lesser error, and it is able to be corrected by incorporation into a sound philosophy of nature. Genuine scientists do not carry their material-ist or empiricist methodology to the point of denying natural forms. Generally, indeed, though they are not explicit Aristotelians, they rather have an implicit common sense based natural philosophy.

A rationalist science or philosophy of nature, however, like that of the Idealists, has to be simply rejected. This tendency is to be found in every period. But particularly did it get out of hand during the first millennium of the Christian era. As already noted, however, the philosophical influence of Platonism had a lot to do with this.

It is not being argued here that the founders of modern science were wrong to reject the excesses of the particular formalism and rationalism distinctive of the pre-modern era. In fact the processes of rejection were already under way in the late mediaeval period. The modern philosophers of science, therefore, should be given credit for carrying this scientific revolution through. Thus was re-stored to their proper places in the investigation of nature the em-pirical role of the senses and the fundamental role of explanation in terms of material causality. We have put this as the re-naturalization of nature, a recovery of natural realism.

We wish to argue, however, that the circumstances attending this most important change in the history of science did not allow it to issue in a balanced view of science. It was a necessary correction – but it ended in the adoption of a flawed philosophy of nature. It rightly rejected one extreme but fell into the other if, from the point of view of natural science, one not as fatal to genuine scientific achievements as the rationalistic error it supplanted.

The way this presented itself was as a rejection of Aristotle's philosophy as a whole, taking the form of a wholesale rejection of his philosophy and science. It is important to understand, however, that it was at first only the rejection of his philosophy of nature, which was the same as his natural science. To characterize it simply as an anti-metaphysical move at the beginning is to misread the significance of the change. Descartes himself believed he was doing Metaphysics, even if he had inherited a notion of metaphysics that had become distorted in late scholasticism (by medium of the influence of Suarez).

A fundamental subjectivism and rationalism at the metaphysical level had already entered into scholastic metaphysics which was to lead to the rejection of formal and final causes. But it was precisely the rejection of Aristotle's notion of science and causality in the natural order that "cut loose" modern science from its antecedents. This in turn meant the rejection of any realistic notion of metaphysics, a process that was begun by the British empiricists and completed in Kant.

One must not, however, confuse the process of philosophical speculation that marks modern philosophy with the way modern science viewed its scientific task. In the result the modern scientist saw what he was doing as an intensive investigation into the fundamental elements of things combined with the mathematical modeling of the quantitative order of such elements hidden within bodies. This latter side of the scientific endeavour gives to the whole object of science a mechanistic as opposed to a purely materialistic character, and enables the scientist to feel that somehow the human mind is able ultimately to master nature.

This "formal" side of the work of modern science did tend to complicate the scientist's understanding of what he was doing. But, and this is the aspect we wish to highlight, it is the reductive line of explanation in material terms which becomes the "substantive" one and in particular determines the direction of the search for an ultimate explanation of things in modern scientific terms.

Putting the more sophisticated aspects of the project of modern science aside, let us now examine it simply in terms of Aristotle's division of the four causes. There are actually five causes. For in any production the formal type cause has to operate in two ways, one intrinsic and the other extrinsic. As the latter it is called the exemplary cause.

Following Aristotle's way of presenting the causes, in terms of an artificial thing, we can take the example of a house or building. In order to explain why a house exists we must take into account five lines of explanation, the building materials (material cause), the structure of the building (formal cause), the builder (efficient cause), the idea or plan of the building (exemplary cause) and the end or reason for the building (final cause). Take away any one of these causal influences and there can be no building. Nor can the reason for the existence of the building be fully understood. It will be noticed that two of the causal influences are intrinsic (material and formal) and the other three extrinsic (efficient, exemplary and final). One may suspect at this point that there may be some connection here with the five ways or proofs for the existence of God. But we will come to that shortly.

Now Aristotle does not wish us to remain with the example. It is only that the various kinds of causal influence can be understood easily in relation to a work of art rather than a work of nature. But the same necessity of there being such causal lines of explanation applies to the case of natural things, indeed of anything whose existence is not self explanatory. Our understanding of the reasons for bodily things in the physical universe remains incomplete if we are not able to identify one or other of these causal influences upon their existence (which may in fact be the case in many instances).

There are two ways in which we can have a relatively complete understanding of natural things (bodily substances) which falls short of a perfect understanding. The first is where we limit our investigation to the intrinsic causes, and express our notions in logical terms. In fact our own human nature is the only case (in the order of substance) in which this gives us a clear and specific (distinct) understanding. In the case of all other natural things we can only acquire a general understanding (of the genus) with our knowledge of the species of the thing completed in a round about way by consideration of the distinctive accidents of the thing.

The second refers to our use of all the lines of explanation but with our investigation limited to what is called the level of "second causes". That is to say we do not go to the ultimate level of efficient, exemplary and final causality, but are satisfied with proximate or immediate causal influences. This is the way the natural philosopher and natural scientist proceeds. The reasoning to a first cause, supreme exemplar and last final cause takes one beyond the physical order and into that of the metaphysical. But since all our understanding has to begin in the sensible and physical order of things we understand things first at the level of second causes.

Now it may be seen that in substantial and intrinsic terms the modern scientific method dispenses with all but the material cause and in so far as it allows recourse to extrinsic causes allows it only to secondary efficient causes. There is thus a recognition of the need for an explanation in terms of efficient causality but it is affected by the overriding influence of the material line of explanation so that it is rather understood in terms of pre-existing material conditions. We have seen also that there is a use of formal causality but it is not properly intrinsic to the substance and it too is affected by the over-riding influence of the material line of explanation. As noted above, the formal line of explanation is confined to the order of quantity.

In the end we have the overriding thrust of the modern scientific endeavour to explain things by reducing them to their ultimate material elements. The natural urge of the mind to go as far as one can in understanding the causes of things presses the modern mind to do this along the only line of explanation it knows, as it were, and to find the ultimate elements into which a natural body can be divided. That way it is believed we may reach a "theory of everything".

The problem with this however is twofold. Firstly, there is no possibility of reaching an ultimate indivisible particle. For, as Aristotle has demonstrated, bodies or material things are intrinsically composite – not as conceived mathematically, but as conceived physically. This composition cannot be detected by sensible or measurable means but has to be seen intellectually. For neither substantial form nor primary matter are "things" or bodily substances in their own right.

The second aspect of the problem is that the line of material causality goes in the direction of pure potency (primary matter) and so rather than such a line of explanation giving us a clearer vision of things it descends into a world of less and less intelligibility. Indeed, the "ideal" limit of this line of "explanation" is nothingness. It is significant that as the scientists feel they are close to having a theory of everything by this route there are some who begin seriously to believe that everything not merely can be explained ultimately as coming from nothing, but must be so explained.

We may say that this, though absurd, is indeed the only logical alternative to belief in God as the first cause, supreme being and ultimate explanation of everything (other than God). For the path to an ultimate understanding of things actually existing has to be upward to higher and higher levels of act, not downwards to the lowest depths of pure potency. That is not to deny the usefulness of analysis of the material kind. But even its masters have realized that the empirical method, which is from the order of material causality, when combined with the mathematical, which is tied to quantity, the first property of things by reason of their matter, is ordered not to understanding so much as of the ability to use things (of the "how" rather than the "why").

What is missing in the modern approach then are the lines of explanation or causality that lie not on the side of potentiality or matter but on the side of actuality or form (principally substantial form). The modern approach is equivalent to explaining the existence of a house in terms only of the materials brought onto the site so that somehow these materials by some inexplicable "force" arrange themselves into the completed building. Of course, in the case of an artefact taken as a whole such as a house all the other causes are clearly accounted for by the existence and action of the human agent necessarily involved as maker, designer and user.

It is important to point out here that though the existence of one building needs to be attributed ultimately to one maker, according to the idea of one designer and for the sake of one user, its execution generally involves a host of subordinate workers and its use may be had by many delegate users or tenants. So one observing the construction and occupation of the building may never see the principal builder and architect, nor its owner. Nonetheless, the influence of these superior causes upon the existence of the house will be clearly understood to be necessary. It is no argument against the application of this analysis of the various kinds of causality by analogy to the existence of things in nature that the first efficient cause, the original exemplary cause and the final cause are all invisible. All these influences will be visible in natural activities at the level of second causes.

It is true that the substantial forms of things below man are not knowable specifically except through their actions and other accidents. In this regard then it is not easy to distinguish the formal/substantial line of explanation from the material/ accidental. Similarly, apart from ourselves, it is not possible to identify distinctly the final cause of a natural species, as for instance dolphins. But the accidents and parts of things have to be understood formally and finally if they are to be properly dealt with. The actions and parts of things have a distinct finality, more easily recognizable as one goes up the scale of being. The organs of living things, for instance, cannot be properly understood without reference to the ends or objects they are ordered to.

Nor can the faculties of sense knowledge in animals be understood without taking into account differences of form and finality. The eye is for the sake of seeing light and colours, the ear for hearing sounds and so on. Such is obvious enough but there is a complex of senses both external and internal in the higher animals and man that demands close study and discrimination of forms and ends. How is sense consciousness to be distinguished from seeing and hearing? What distinguishes imagination from sensation? What are the differences between memory as it functions in man and in other animals? What is meant by intelligence in dolphins as opposed to intelligence in human beings?

None of these sorts of questions can be answered though mere observation and measurement. For such a materialistically oriented approach cannot bring out the fine distinctions required to be made. Room must be made for an intellectual insight that grasps the forms or essences of things. This is done masterfully by St. Thomas in his commentaries on Aristotle's two "minor" works, "On Sense and the Sensible" and "On Memory and Reminiscence".

The poverty of the modern scientific approach may be seen in the treatment of sleep and dreams, where from a failure to understand their distinctive forms and proper functions it becomes impossible to discriminate the normal from the abnormal or the healthy from the pathological. So it is that much so-called scientific or experimental psychology produces a distorted explanation of the human psyche (as in Freud) and the practice of psychiatry based on such "science" can do more harm than good to the patients, and that not just mentally but also morally.

Sleep, as Aristotle explained it, is a natural binding of the "common sense", i.e. of sense consciousness. That is to say it is a temporary suspension of the activity of this internal sense. Its "form" is then understood even though it is the absence of activity. Its final cause is also able to be seen clearly as being for the sake of the animal's health, by rest and recuperation.

Moliere famously ridiculed this reference to intrinsic powers in his play *Le Malade Imaginaire*, saying that a (scholastic) philosopher would explain why opium puts people to sleep by mentioning the fact that it has a 'dormitive virtue'. That is an explanation in terms of formal cause. But it is only a case of supplying the name to the intrinsic principle. If people are prone to sleep regularly that indicates there is something in their bodily make-up which accounts for this. If a drug has a similar effect it at least identifies the property of the drug. But the positing of a formal or intrinsic power in this case is no different from saying that fire causes heat in things because it has caloric virtue (heat), which other things do not have.

This is a start to investigating more fully what such a physical quality is. It is not meant to stand alone without further definition and explication in terms of material cause, which the modern scientist excels in. To posit the existence of formal causes is not as silly as denying their existence and suggesting that the language of powers and virtues is meaningless. A great many of the modern philosophers who mock the scholastics in this regard themselves indulge in an empty rationalism that outdoes the worst kind of nominalistic logicism of the late scholastics.

However, we are more concerned here with ultimate formal (exemplary) and final causes than with causes generally, to show that there are lines of explanation other than in terms of empirical investigations of "phenomena" (material causality) which in its modern application makes use of "formal" mathematical modelling grounded in quantitative relations. This (mixed) scientific method does not necessarily exclude what by contrast are called philosophical methods, but it is generally promoted as doing so.

We have seen how the modern scientific method, so conceived as exclusive, cannot in principle provide an ultimate explanation, so that the search for a "theory of everything" along these lines must forever remain without success. In fact, besides leading to a dead-end it is a distraction from looking for such an explanation in the proper places. The descent into matter is a movement towards pure potency and indeterminancy, and ultimately would come down to nothing, if that were possible. Of course, pure potency or primary matter is not nothing and so indirectly can be a path to the actual source of all being. In fact, motion, or physical change, which is the level of activity present only in material reality, is one of the facts from which Aristotle and St. Thomas reason to the ultimate explanation of all reality. But the starting point has to be something actual not purely potential, which motion is, being, as Aristotle defines it, "the act of the potential as it is potential". It is only in so far as something is still potential, as water is to heat until it reaches it boiling point, that it can be said to be in the process of change from one state of actuality to another.

In order to explain this process of change or motion it is necessary to go outside the thing in the process of change or in motion.

For what is potential in any respect does not explain its passing to a state of actuality, as is clearly seen in the example. The potential, as such, does not actualize itself. Hence, the existence of motion presupposes the existence of an agent, i.e. something actually (or virtually, which means having a higher degree of actuality which subsumes the form concerned, as an animal is not a plant but has the powers of doing what plants do) that is responsible for the movement from being potentially so to being actually so. Taking this in its most general and essential sense, it means that whilstever there is potentiality in the thing concerned there needs to be another actual thing to explain its level of the actuality according to that potential.

This cannot go on indefinitely or by a circular process. So the process of motion cannot be explained unless we posit a being without it, which can account for it. That is the notion of something absolutely changeless and unchangeable, or in the language of Aristotle, an unmoved (and unmoveable) being; something of pure actuality of being and not potential in any respect. That is the metaphysical notion of Pure Act, which is what is meant by God. The English word "mover" can be misleading in this regard. For its notion refers us to something that of itself can move before it does move. But there is no "can move" in the notion of the absolutely first agent. (We use the Latin based word "motor" is the same way; for it means only what can move, if we are more focused on it when it is actually causing motion)

The actual English word that would correspond to what is intended to be signified here would be a literal equivalent of the Latin word *movens*, i.e. movent. It is difficult for us to get this pure notion for in our experience even when natural movents act they are in some way also moved to act (which is the basis of the second way of Aristotle and St. Thomas). But in the case of the absolutely first "mover" it must be said that even in creating things God is not moved. God acts without change in himself. The action of God is of an altogether opposite quality to all that is within our experience. This really confirms the proof from motion – for our experience is of things in which there is always some potentiality and the argument has led to a being in which there is none.

So we are already embarked upon the process of reasoning from potentiality to actuality, as opposed to endeavouring to explain things by analysis actual things into their most elementary parts or potential principles. As already noted, according to St. Thomas, there are at least five ways in which the former reasoning can proceed. And these happen to be along the five lines of causality outlined above. Matter and form are intrinsic causes, or reasons (principles of understanding), of bodies, which are the things which come immediately within our experience. The other three, efficient cause, exemplary cause and final cause are obviously extrinsic to the same things.

These three are easily related to the second, fourth and fifth proofs for the existence of God presented by St. Thomas. But how can we relate the first and third ways to matter and form? So far as matter is concerned, this in fact has already been done above in the discussion of the proof from motion, which though not directly from matter is from that "act" which belongs to material things in so far as they are material. It should not be forgotten, however, that where bodies are concerned motion is in the accidental order and is not limited to local motion, but extends to the other two kinds of change, qualitative (called alteration) and quantitative (called growth). Local motion is indeed the flimsiest kind of change and the proof is best presented in terms of qualitative change.

So far as (substantial) form is concerned, again the proof does not proceed from the form as such but from the nature of the "act" of existence which flows to material things from their (material) forms. That is to say it is from the contingent nature of bodily existence. There is nothing more obvious than that bodies, though they have existence, are inherently bound to cease to exist at any time. They do not exist necessarily (which means they cannot cease to be) but contingently (which means they can cease to be).

Thus, since their very existence is not had from within themselves, if they do have existence, it must be from without. Here again one cannot go on indefinitely arguing to another being which itself is dependent in its existence. For, just as not everybody can be a debtor, so there must exist some original thing that "owns" existence and therefore must be the source of the possession of it in those that do not. This thing of independent wealth of being will be understood as rich in a manner quite opposite to creditors in our experience, whose wealth, no matter how great, is inevitably finite. From a position of infinite wealth of existence no bestowal of existence upon others can possibly diminish the owner's store of wealth.

This aspect of God in this proof confirms the unchangeability that was deduced in the first way. It may be noted, too, that the analogy passes to one of gift rather than loan where spiritual beings are concerned. For, such is the generosity of the owner/creditor that he does not intend that the "loan" be ever paid back (except in an act of gratitude).

It will be noted that in these two proofs, the concepts of motion or change and contingency strictly taken apply only to the physical and material order of things. Thus taken motion is the kind of activity or action proper to bodies. It is accidental and transitory. Some raise the objection that though the proof leads to an unmoved mover it does not necessarily lead to God. For the motion or change belonging to bodies is not to be found in purely spiritual beings (such as an angels, or spiritual souls).

Similarly, it may be argued that the concept of contingency used by St. Thomas is peculiar to corruptible bodies. He even uses the language of necessary being in reference to angels etc. Again this kind of contingency is not to be found in purely spiritual beings less than God. So it is not sufficient for a proof for the existence of God.

It may be said that these two arguments (the first and the third) are not complete without a further demonstration that there is a kind of change even in the order of spiritual creatures and that there is a kind of contingency also even there. Indeed, in regard to the proof from contingency St. Thomas seems to have to rely on an appeal to the second proof to complete it, by showing that the "necessity" of the existence of spirits is still a caused one and thus requires an uncaused cause to account for it.

However, though there are two stages involved it seems better to say that the notions of change and contingency, despite being taken from the material world, lead naturally by analogy to their extension to all created things. For there is motion or change in spiritual activity in as much as angels have thoughts and choices that do not belong to their substance. With regard to the notion of contingency, the angels' substantial existence, though naturally necessary and everlasting (there being no intrinsic propensity for non-existence in it), is not absolutely necessary, as it is always dependent upon God. Taken in their full and extended senses, then, the two proofs lead to having to posit the existence of God.

When we come to the remaining three proofs, the notions from which we start, though also taken from the physical material world of our sense experience, have immediate metaphysical significance (extending to the spiritual). For the terms involved, efficiency (power), perfection (truth) and finality (goodness) are from the start analogous. To a Christian, indeed, they also are remote indications of the Trinity in God. Not that they are rational proofs of the Trinity (which is not possible) but they are congruent with such truth given the knowledge we have from Faith.

We do not intend to go into the details of these three last proofs as this would make this article too long. They can be the subject of another essay/article. It is sufficient to notice that, like the other two, they lead to positing a being of absolutely opposite kind to those from which the argument proceeds; from dependence upon causality to independence; from imperfection in being to absolute perfection; from being essentially ordered to something beyond itself to being beyond all subordination.

In presentation these lines of ultimate explanation may cross over at times. But the lines of causality are clearly distinguished. They all involve a passage from the objects of our experience, having in some way or other the limitations of potentiality in their different forms of actuality, to a being that has no such limitation whatsoever. The general line of explanation in ultimate terms then ought to be upwards to the actualizing causal influences made so evident, rather than downwards into the depths of matter where, taken by itself, things only get more and more indeterminate and obscure. There is a "theory of everything" but the modern scientist is looking in the wrong place, and employing a means that has a different use.

One final point: The discovery of the ultimate explanation(s) for reality as we know it only enables us to accept as true the proposition that God exists. And the notion of God involved has to be taken though relation, and by way of opposition, to what comes within the range of our understanding. It does not mean that we have any insight into the inner nature of the divine being. The God of the philosophers remains an unknown God, a distant thing, someone personal no doubt, but beyond the possibility of our personal acquaintance.

Christian revelation changes all that. But, on the one hand, we have to be very careful to avoid the impression that we have by reason reached a knowledge of God as revealed by Faith. It is the same God but the proofs of his existence (and even providential governance) as the author of nature are quite distinct from the knowledge we have of God as the author of grace. On the other hand, the Christian can tend to disdain such an impoverished notion of God as is to be had by reason and consequently to deny the value of the proofs. This is a grave mistake. For it is the failure to promote the true lines of ultimate explanation, or the genuine "theory of everything", that allows a materialistic and atheistic explanation to be presented (and almost universally accepted nowadays) as if it were the only one possible.

Appendix B

De Lubac on Grace and Nature:
Reflections Prompted by Defense of de Lubac
by Nicholas J. Healy III

Nicholas Healy's article helps to clarify de Lubac's position and counters some criticisms of it. However, in my judgment, on the one hand, it fails to address the basic errors in the arguments made by de Lubac in regard to the understanding itself of the notion of "natural desire" as related to grace and the beatific vision; and, on the other hand, it fails to properly interpret the texts of Aquinas that de Lubac claims support what he holds on the question. The errors are to do with a failure to note the necessary distinction between a natural desire or inclination that follows upon form had and one that refers to a natural desire or proportion in matter for form that bespeaks only a receptivity. This mistake, however, leads to a more basic misunderstanding of the nature of a passive potency and in particular obediential potency. This necessarily results in a misreading of the texts of Aquinas.

The essay of Healy to which we refer is that entitled "*Henri de Lubac on Nature and Grace: A Note on Some Recent Contributions to the Debate*".[1] Healy gives a resounding defense of de Lubac's po-

---

[1] Nicholas J. Healy, "Henri de Lubac on Nature and Grace: A Note on Some Recent Contributions to the Debate". *Communio: International Catholic Review* 35 (Winter 2008): 535-64.

sition on the relation between grace and nature. He clarifies de Lubac's position so as to avoid much criticism of what he says. Indeed, one has to concede some of his points against the critics of de Lubac. Yet, our view is that in the end he does not succeed in absolving de Lubac of the fundamental error of his position. We say this in the context of the comment by Lonergan:

"De Lubac was just mixed up on this point. He isn't satisfactory on it. De Lubac says it has an exigence and it does not have an exigence ... While de Lubac is a man of extraordinary erudition and also respected as a very holy man by people who have lived with him in his own Province, he is not a competent speculative thinker. At least I don't find that in him. The way he tried to handle the question of exigence shows that.[2]"

Indeed, in defending his basic position de Lubac expressed himself in language that in reality made significant and fundamental concessions to the view he was opposing. Healy uses these concessions to counter some of the criticism made against de Lubac. We will endeavour to identify these inconsistencies and even contradictory statements but, more importantly, to expose the cause of his mixed up thinking on the matter.

The source of the intellectual problem he had we may at this point put in very general terms as a problem of theological method in dealing with what are in essence purely philosophical aspects of

---

[2] Bernard Lonergan, "Phenomenology and Logic: The Boston Lectures on Mathematical Logic and Existentialism", in *Collected Works of Bernard Lonergan*, vol. 18, ed. P. McShane (University of Toronto Press, 2001), 350.

the question under discussion. The weakness in his treatment is from a lack of sound Metaphysics, or even of a proper grasp of the role of theoretical or speculative thinking. This leads to a heavy reliance upon "concrete" concepts and practical judgments in dealing with the necessary distinctions to be made and conclusions to be drawn. His misapplication of the distinction between human nature in the concrete and in the abstract is clear evidence of this.

In suffering from this intellectual malaise he was not alone. Indeed, one could say that it is the common trait of the modern mind since theoretical truth was consigned to the narrow field of the particular sciences (mathematics, physico-mathematics and the natural sciences) thereby excluding all intellectual value from Metaphysics. Philosophy has now become separated from "Science", reduced to our trying to cope with the practical order of human affairs (with no theoretical support).

That, however, is a comment upon the general state of modern philosophy. What compounds this problem in the case of theologians is that they tend to approach what are the metaphysical dimensions of a question that has implications in theology first from a theological standpoint, when what should be done first is clarify the philosophical dimensions of the problem under consideration. The "new theologians" are handicapped in this regard because they lack a grounding in Metaphysics; indeed they see any appeal to abstract "theoretical" knowledge as somehow aligned with Cartesian and Kantian rationalism.

This is not to say that it is always a defect in theological method not to put rational or natural considerations before those of grace and faith; it only is so when dealing with questions in sacred theology which come also within the range of reason. Adopting the right order of procedure is particularly important today when there is such a weakness in Metaphysics in many theologians. Thomist theologians should be able to take for granted a sound foundation in philosophy. In matters strictly of supernatural faith, above reason altogether, of course, one only uses reason or natural considerations in a secondary way, as St. Thomas explains[3] (this consideration needs to be brought into play also when discussing St. Thomas's use of reason based upon natural desire to defend the reasonableness of belief in the supernatural nature of our ultimate end – see discussion below).

In this particular question de Lubac demonstrates a defective notion of nature, which notion is, of course, central to the whole issue. He believes that God could have created a human nature without grace, but that nature would then be not just in a different state but would be somehow without an inclination or desire for the beatific vision that belongs to it naturally. That is to say, it would lack what belongs to it by its very nature.

But, if the desire for the beatific vision is natural, that is to say, present in idea and reality before grace is had, then it must be present in any state in which human nature is created, with or without grace, and would remain forever present even though grace was never accorded to it. This is what is contradicted by de Lubac as brought out by Healy's explanation:

---

[3] Thomas Aquinas. *Summa Theologiae.* I, 32, 1 ad 2.

"De Lubac's natural desire for the supernatural is not grace; it is not the supernatural effect of the actual call to the beatific vision. It is, rather, the natural *infrastructure* placed by God in intellectual nature *for the sake of realizing his plan* to bestow the call to supernatural happiness in a second "moment" that is logically and ontologically distinct with respect to the act of creating intellectual nature in the first place.[4]" (italics added)

That is to say, God has placed this "natural desire" for the beatific vision in human nature because of his plan to raise man to supernatural happiness, i.e. because of his plan to endow human nature with grace, and, if he did create man without this positive ordination to the beatific vision, there would not be any reason in human nature for such a "natural desire".

This is to have two versions of human nature, and this is to not understand the very meaning of nature. As the same considerations of the relation between grace and nature apply also to the angels, this would mean that there would have to be two versions of each angel. In truth, however, there can be only one act or "moment" of creation whereby human nature is created together with all its natural inclinations or desires.

De Lubac appeals to the distinction between nature understood in the abstract, or "hypothetically", and understood in the concrete, or in fact. But, that is to further distort our understanding of nature. Hypothesis rather pertains to the order of existence than to the order of essence or nature. De Lubac here, as elsewhere, mixes up the

---

[4]Healy, "Nature and Grace", 553.

essential and the existential. A nature may have two modes of exist-ence, but it is absurd to say that it can have two modes of substantial form or essence, one with a fundamentally natural desire for the be-atific vision and one without.

De Lubac is endeavouring, as we shall see, to make a distinction that has to do with some sort of inclination to our ultimate end. But, he leans too far towards thinking of the relationship of our being to the supernatural end in natural terms understood in the ordinary sense, i.e. as an inclination following a form had, something that is quite ironic considering his criticisms of Garrigou-Lagrange and others.

When expressing such criticism, de Lubac demonstrates a gross idea of nature in purely physical terms instead of in metaphysical terms, a mistake that an Aristotelian would not make, but which one would if one's mind is too tied to modern physico-mathematical science, as Jesuit thinkers tend to be. It is this mistak-en "naturalistic" idea of nature, which Garrigou-Lagrange does not suffer from, that underlies the intellectual fallacy of secularism, but de Lubac then tries to accuse the "Neo-thomist" school of fostering.

The phrase "natural desire" has obviously to be taken analogous-ly and to such an extent that it borders on being taken equivocally. However, this will be examined more closely below. That, then, is a preliminary view of the cause of de Lubac's unsuccessful attempt to resolve the problem of the relation between nature and grace or be-tween the natural and the supernatural.

As a matter of method, as noted it is a mistake to address the question of nature on the supposition that grace has been given. It is necessary first to clarify our understanding of the meaning of nature before bringing in the additional question of grace and the relation between grace and nature. That is to say, one should begin the examination of this whole question on the supposition that grace is not given. Part of the whole problem in de Lubac's argument is that he insists that the question is to be approached only on the supposition of grace being had. But, let us go through Healy's defence of de Lubac's position to substantiate what we say.

Firstly, however, we should note the places where Healy does counter somewhat the criticisms made of de Lubac in regard to this question. Stephen Long, it seems, has accused de Lubac of a too exclusive concentration on the texts of St. Thomas that appear to support his position. Healy quite effectively, we believe, shows that this is not a fair criticism. On the basis of his work there is no reason to question de Lubac's academic integrity in his struggle to reconcile texts of St. Thomas on the matter, which are on all accounts difficult to reconcile.

There seems no doubt that de Lubac was a marvellous and meticulous scholar and took into account anything and everything he could in trying to solve an intellectual problem, especially one of such a profound nature as this. Indeed, in positive theology his work is of the highest order and nothing said here is meant to reflect on his genius, if you like, in such like fields.

Another point of criticism, noted by Healy, is one made by Feingold. This will provide us the opportunity to expound our own understanding of the meaning to be placed upon the "natural desire" for the beatific vision. Healy puts it in this way:

"A third objection to de Lubac has been formulated with particular clarity by Lawrence Feingold:

'For St. Thomas, the possession of a certain form determines a relation to a given natural end that is called for by that form ... [cf. SCG III, c. 150] From this he concludes that a new supernatural form—grace—must be "super-added" to human nature so that it can be ordered to an end that is "above human nature" ... This clearly implies that human nature in itself without grace is not naturally or essentially ordered (and cannot be fittingly ordered) to an end that is above human nature.

If this new form, which determines us to a supernatural end, is above our nature, then this supernatural finality is not to be said to be imprinted in our nature itself. Nor can the finality that is generated by this supernatural form be considered to be an "essential finality." It is ultimately contradictory to suppose that our nature itself—without the addition of a supernatural principle—could be intrinsically determined by a supernatural finality, or have a supernatural finality inscribed upon it, or have an "essential finality" that is supernatural. If this were the case, our nature itself would be in some sense supernatural'."[5]

Healy's response is as follows:

"There are two points to make in response to this objection. First, the idea that the final end of nature is determined by its form is simply another way of asserting that the final end of nature must be essentially proportionate to nature, or that nature can attain its final end by its own abilities. Aquinas explicitly and repeatedly rejects this principle as applicable to the question of the final end of

---

[5]Healy, "Nature and Grace", 560.

human nature: "Even though by his nature man is inclined to his ultimate end he cannot reach it by nature but only by grace, and this owing to the loftiness of that end." [*In Boethius de Trinitate*, q. 6, a. 4 ad 5; see also ST I-II, q. 91, a. 4 ad 3; q. 109,a. 4 ad 2; *De Veritate*, q. 8, a. 3 ad 12; q. 24 a. 10 ad 1; and *De Malo*, q. 5, a. 1.] The same teaching is repeated in *Summa theologiae* I-II, q. 5, a. 5, where the second objection reads: "Since man is more noble than irrational creatures, it seems that he must be better equipped than they. But irrational creatures can attain their end by their natural powers. Much more therefore can man attain beatitude by his natural powers." Aquinas responds:

The nature that can attain perfect good, although it needs help from without in order to attain it, is of more noble condition than a nature which cannot attain perfect good, but attains some imperfect good, although it need no help from without in order to attain it .... And therefore the rational creature, which can attain the perfect good of beatitude, but needs the divine assistance for the purpose, is more perfect than the irrational creature, which is not capable of attaining this good, but attains some imperfect good by its natural powers.

The text that Feingold appeals to (SCG III, c. 150) provides an account of the divine assistance that fittingly and efficaciously orders human nature to supernatural beatitude by means of the additional form of grace. It does not support Feingold's assertion that the super-added form of grace gives nature a new final end."[6]

---

[6]Healy, "Nature and Grace", 560-61.

The text of SCG III, c. 150 contains:

Amplius. Unumquodque ordinatur in finem sibi convenientem secundum rationem suae formae: diversarum enim specierum diversi sunt fines. Sed finis in quem homo dirigitur per auxilium divinae gratiae, est supra naturam humanam. Ergo oportet quod homini superaddatur aliqua supernaturalis forma et perfectio, per quam convenienter ordinetur in finem praedictum.

"Further, every thing is ordered to the end suitable to it according to the reason of its form. For the ends of diverse species are diverse. But the end to which man is directed through the help of divine grace is above human nature. Therefore it is necessary that some supernatural form and perfection be added to man, through which he may be ordered to the aforesaid end." (translation mine)

It must be said that here Healy has fudged the issue. There is no escaping the necessary connection between form and end. Indeed, Aristotle's use of the word "entelechy" for form means "end had within". The inclination following form had is precisely to the thing's "suitable end". What does not have a necessary connection with end is matter, and as we shall see, the "natural desire" for a supernatural end, though not in matter, since this principle is purely physical, is an inclination that more appropriately is applied to a purely potential metaphysical principle.

The help provided by grace is by way of supernatural form, by which only is one ordered to the supernatural end, but that supposes some "material" or purely potential principle had by the nature so raised to a supernatural level of being. That is the real solution to the question and it is what de Lubac and Healy are mixed up about.

If one reads "by his nature man is inclined to his ultimate [supernatural] end" as referring to an inclination following form had, then that form has to be the supernatural form of grace. This plainly contradicts what St. Thomas says in SCG III, 150. But, if one reads the inclination as other than following form had, but as belonging to what is "material" or potential only, it can still be a natural inclination (appetite or desire) within human (spiritual) nature and there is no contradiction.

The resolution of this problem is we believe to be found in making the above distinction in the meaning of natural desire in a created substance. The root of the difficulty lies in not making the proper distinctions between active and passive inclinations, that is between inclinations following upon forms or acts, and inclinations (also called appetites and desires) pertaining only to what is purely potential, like that of primary matter for form. The natural inclination or desire within human nature as referred to by St. Thomas in relation to the supernatural end has to be first located within the substance of human beings. But here there are two kinds of natural inclinations, that of form for matter, or act for potency and that of matter for form or of pure potency for form as its act.

How, then, are we to interpret St. Thomas's use of the phrase "natural desire" in relation to our supernatural end or ultimate happiness? More immediately it is a natural desire for grace(as for form), and only consequentially for the beatific vision(as for corresponding end), whose attainment has to involve supernatural powers. Now within a created substance or nature there are only intrinsic inclinations or proportions, such as substantial form or spiritual soul in human nature, which is an inclination or proportion for

primary matter, or its material body, and primary matter or material body, which is an inclination or proportion for substantial form,
or its spiritual soul. These are real so called natural appetites or desires.

However, there are higher, or deeper, inclinations or proportions
(of act to potency and vice versa) within human being, and these are
the proportions of essence (as human substance) to existence (human esse), and vice versa. These, too, can be described as natural in
the metaphysical (boethian) sense of nature. The inclination or proportion, that is essence within the very being (ens) of human beings,
is naturally a proportion only to created existence. Relative to existence, however, essence is pure potency, a pure receptivity for existence, so that it should not be conceived as having in itself any existence (esse). But, once existence is received according to this essence
or nature (as substance) it then has an inclination to act through its
powers, as a natural inclination following the form or essence had.
This consequential inclination needs to be carefully distinguished
from the inclination or proportion that defines it in relation to its
substantial existence (esse).

We know from Revelation that deep within the human being
there must lie a potency or capacity, and hence a desire, for grace (as
divine esse participated), since it has been activated. It would be impossible for God to give grace to anything if there were no capability
in it to receive it, as, for instance, to a tree. For, grace has the nature
of act or form. Only in God does act exist without being received
into potency. Nor can this potency or capacity be created separately
and placed in nature, for then it would have to have its own form

and existence, which is to say it would already be grace (that is a problem for de Lubac's position).

Moreover, this supposition would involve an infinite process of having to provide a capacity for the reception of the new potency inserted. This potential or capacity, it is to be noted, is primarily in the created substance or nature as entity (ens) and only consequently in the powers of intellect and will which belong to the accidental order.

Now this is where we need to bring in the notion of obediential potency. The desire cannot be given any quality of act or formality. It is not an inclination following form but, like primary matter, the sort of inclination pertaining to pure potency. Like matter it has to be entirely receptive or purely passive. But, as we have noted, it transcends the passivity and receptivity even of primary matter. For, it signifies a receptivity for an act of form (esse) that not only is above the human but is above all natural and created existence. It is a receptivity or potentiality belonging to spiritual essences and forms for the divine. It is a natural inclination in the sense that it is necessarily to be found in every thing spiritual whether or not it is actualized.

And it can only be actualized by the action of an agent superior to the natural level of the patient. It is not a natural passivity in the usual sense where action and passion are on the same natural level. We can use an analogy here but it has to be carefully detached from conditions that belong to the natures of things. A pen or pencil has the capacity or power of writing a poem. But, it does not belong to the nature of ink or lead to do so. How then can we say that the pen or pencil has this power? It does so only under the power of the poet and that only whilst the poet is acting. As soon as the poet ceases to compose the poem immediately the pen or pencil loses its instrumental or subordinate power and activity.

The creation of a poem is something that can only be natural to a being of spiritual form, or rational nature. Does the poet confer this power on the pen or pencil? Yes, as a form or quality but only whilst writing the poem. It is the higher agent that is conferring an active but transitory power. But, this supposes that the pen or pencil had the capacity to be so elevated. This means that it must have had already the passive potential to be used to write the poem. This receptivity is not natural to it in the ordinary sense. It is only a rational being that has the natural power of writing a poem. But it can transmit something of this to a lower form of being.

Thus, we have to carefully distinguish the natural/rational power to write poetry, which is actually conferred on the pen or pencil in the act of writing according to the receptive capacity or passive potential in the pen and pencil to be so raised to that kind of activity. The pen or pencil is actually writing the poem as well as the poet. But, just lying on the desk the pen does not have this kind of power. Still it must have in it the capacity to be so used. That is obediential power. By itself it does nothing in regard to poetizing, nor does it have the power to do so from the nature of its ink or lead. Indeed, the same ink and lead might exist without ever being brought into such a kind of activity, and it would not complain that it has been denied its natural end.

So too a human being could be created by God and not raised to the level of active power, form or act, that is grace so as to be able to enjoy the same sort of divine existence as God. If so (we know otherwise from Revelation) such a human being (or angel) would have no complaint (let alone a right to do so) that he or she had been denied his or her natural happiness – he would not even be aware of the possibility of this supernatural happiness. This is despite the fact such a human being would still have the natural desire for supernatural happiness in the way described. (This is what de Lubac cannot grasp – he cannot detach this natural desire from final possession of the supernatural end)

Just as the capacity in ink or lead to be elevated to the active power of writing poetry does not mean that ink or lead as such is made for that end, so the natural desire for happiness, as obediential, does not determine the human soul in any way to the supernatural end. For that one needs the active power conferred by God which is grace – and one only lives the supernatural life and enjoys the end so long as God's gracious action endures. Take away this action, which is a free gift, and the end disappears.

The above quote from SCG III, 150 confirms this:

Unumquodque ordinatur in finem sibi convenientem secundum rationem suae formae: diversarum enim specierum diversi sunt fines. Sed finis in quem homo dirigitur per auxilium divinae gratiae, est supra naturam humanam. Ergo oportet quod homini superaddatur aliqua supernaturalis forma et perfectio, per quam convenienter ordinetur in finem praedictum.

It is apparent that both Healy and Feingold are overlooking something here, namely, that there is something about some creatures that makes them open to such a reception of grace, should God freely be disposed to grant it. This openness does not give such creatures a new ultimate end, nor even an ordination to such – for such grace is required.

Feingold's criticisms here do not hold against the existence of a natural desire for the beatific vision if it is properly understood as detailed above. St. Thomas himself uses the language of "natural desire" in this regard. But this in a way has proved to be an occasion for misunderstanding. For, except in a certain context as referred to below (in the argument given in I, q. 12), "natural" or "desire" cannot be taken in their ordinary senses in the fundamental resolution of this problem. A natural desire ordinarily supposes a natural form had. "Every form is followed by an inclination". Yet, "natural desire" referred to this openness to divine action above the natural order signifies a lack of any formal determination, as is clear from what St. Thomas says.

We have to resort then to another notion of desire that is used, not as related to forms, but as related to what is understood after the fashion of matter, not as related to something actual in some way, but to what is merely potential. St. Thomas talks of matter having a natural appetite for forms. But, as he also points out, it is a "desire" in the nature of receptivity, something purely passive. Nonetheless, it is real not merely logical. It simply means we have to adjust our notion of natural desire to exclude any kind of formal determination or actuality. The attachment to formal determination as the concomitant of natural desire is at the root of the error of de Lubac. The proportion or order to end comes through form or active potency without which passive potency has no order or proportion to end, just as primary matter has no order to natural ends without being actualised by the appropriate natural forms. So without the supernatural form of grace there cannot be any order or proportion to the supernatural end of the beatific vision (as ultimate supernatural happiness).

That appears to be what de Lubac had great difficulty in seeing and all his wrong statements stem from not totally succeeding in escaping this formal or determinative character being inserted into the notion of natural desire. Most likely it can ultimately be traced to Suarez's concept of matter and potency as not "pure", but somehow containing something of form or act – in conceiving potency as imperfect act. Suarez's interpretation of St. Thomas, as is well known, has dominated modern thinking in philosophy, and is not without general influence in modern Catholic theology, particularly in the Jesuit tradition.

The language of formal determination, or active potency, in relation to the natural ordination, by "natural desire", is in fact what Feingold picks up in de Lubac. Healy repeats it quite strikingly, using such strongly definite terms as "natural infrastructure" to describe this "natural desire". Feingold is right in criticising such a conception of inclination or desire for the beatific vision. It can only be present with grace.

But, given the right conception of such a "natural desire", or even natural inclination, as purely passive, Healy's counter has some point. For the "natural desire" for the beatific vision, so understood, is indeed part of the very nature of the creature of spiritual form or essence. The fact that such a desire is for an end that is above nature does not make it contrary to nature, nor does it have any effect upon the natural specific differences pertaining to men or angels (which come from a difference of forms). But, contrary to the thinking of de Lubac and Healy, the existence of such a "desire', as a purely passive potentiality, does not mean that human nature has in fact or in principle any supernatural ultimate end or "finality". Such end comes to human nature only if God positively wills it, and "imprints" grace within it.

When discussing the hypostatic union, Lonergan gives a nice comparison to the kind of potency involved: "Thirdly, we must distinguish between that human essence as a natural potency to its proper act of existence and that same essence as an obediential potency to the hypostatic union".[7] Just as the essence (essentia) of the creature (ens) names a natural potency for its own act of existence (esse), so in Christ the same human essence names an obediential potency for participation in the divine act of existence (esse divinum). The two existences (natural and supernatural) are distinct but in Christ the natural (human) existence (esse humanum) is subsumed into or under the divine.

So we might apply this to the act/form of grace (and act of glory) as it comes to us, with this difference. In the case of Christ the union is in the one person; in us the union is between one human person and a participation in the nature of the trinity of divine persons. Moreover, in the case of Christ, the union is not with an already existing human person, but the (individual) human nature comes into existence only through the union. In the case of the Christian and

---

[7] Bernard Lonergan, "The Ontological and Psychological Constitution of Christ", in *Collected Works of Bernard Lonergan*, vol. 7, eds, M. Shields, F. Crowe S.J., R. Doran S.J. (University of Toronto Press, English translation 2002), 113.

grace, the union presupposes a pre-existing human person (at least ontologically if not chronologically) and grace is to be conceived as an additional "quality" or form, as explained by St. Thomas.

Following Lonergan's analogy, then, just as the human essence (essentia) or nature may be seen as a natural (receptive) potency for the act of existence (esse) in the natural order, thus constituting a natural being (ens), so the same essence (essentia) or nature, or more aptly the whole being (ens), might be seen as an obediential potency for another act of existence (the divine esse participated), thus constituting a graced being, or Christian (natural essence plus substantial existence plus grace, which last is an initial qualitative/luminous participation in the divine esse).

Essentially, the having of grace is the same as the beatific vision, but like with Faith, it is God possessed imperfectly. Thus, the natural desire for grace is the same as the natural desire for ultimate happiness. So it is that when we come to consider the openness to, or most radical potentiality for, the beatific vision, which potentiality "exists" in creatures with spiritual forms or essences, we have to resort to an even deeper and more tenuous notion of natural desire, as pure receptivity to the action of a superior agent.

Indeed, nothing of (additional) formal determination is to be accorded this "capacity for God". The "natural desire" is, therefore, nought else but the created spiritual nature considered as obedient to the supreme divine creative agency, which has the power to make "gods" out of created spirituality no matter how lowly. Indeed, as St. Thomas points out, such is the distance between God and the creature that the grades of spiritual being are as nothing compared to the divine power. Hence Mary, a mere human, has been placed above the highest angels.

Where does this obediential potentiality lie then? In our view it lies in the depths of the very "beingness" (entitas) of the creature of spiritual form or essence. This potentiality is not nothing, for it is a potentiality of the created spiritual essence or being. But it bespeaks nothing additional by way of form or essence considered in itself.

That is where it seems that de Lubac gets caught. For he thinks that it has to be some kind of form of being added to the nature. Hence, he can allow for God, in another providential order, creating a "pure nature" without this natural desire for perfect happiness. What can be added, however, is not this natural desire, but grace as the formal principle of ordination, and the only active ordering, of the creature to the higher perfection by way of participation in divine happiness, otherwise impossible to the created human nature.

Grace is the realisation of this most tenuous of all potentialities. It is a new quality of existence that is endowed upon our nature, a participation in the very be-ing (esse) of God. The "quality" of grace transcends the natural formal order of things, or we might say it "operates" at the level within us of "the form of forms", the act of all acts, existence or esse. All we need to contribute towards the acquisition of this divine "act" is nothing but ourselves as ready, willing and obedient in receiving it.

The other thing to be noted here is that grace provides the "substantial ground" for the "accidental" virtues also required for knowing and loving God. For, perfect happiness consists in the knowledge and love of the three persons in God as they are in themselves. Grace does not make us into God (as Christ himself is) but gives us the active power/light so as to receive in our intellect the divine virtue of Faith (to be transformed into Vision) and in our will the divine virtue of Charity, which is a participation in God's own love.

We know from the nature of intellectual knowledge that our spiritual form is already open naturally to the reception of all other forms. However, this is a natural receptivity (desire) that supposes a natural activity not only on the part of the things known but also of the knower. Aristotle's name for this latter is the agent intellect. But it is better seen as a sort of light of understanding present in us whereby we can come to know what is received from outside us.

In the case of our receptivity to the knowledge of God as he is in himself (themselves), it is grace itself which must provide the light (which becomes the light of glory). As St. Thomas puts it:

"Hinc est quod gratia Dei in Scriptura quasi lux quaedam designatur: dicit enim apostolus Ephes. 5-8: *eratis aliquando tenebrae: nunc autem lux in domino*. Decenter autem perfectio per quam homo promovetur in ultimum finem, quae in Dei visione consistit, dicitur lux, quae est principium videndi." [8] (italics added)

"Hence it is that the grace of God in Scripture is designated as a certain light: for the Apostle says, Ephes. 5-8: *You were sometime darkness: but now light in the Lord*. It is fitting however that the perfection through which man is moved to the ultimate end, which consists in the vision of God, is called light, which is a principle of seeing." (translation mine)

---

[8] Thomas Aquinas. SCG III, c 150.

Grace, therefore, provides not only the "form" or "quality" whereby we are ordered to the beatific vision but also the beginning of the "light" enabling us to see God. What is left on our side (in our nature) to contribute to this possibility? Nothing but what we are, open to the action of the divine agent. The "natural desire" within us before grace has to be emptied of every notion of it proceeding from a positive form or quality ordering us to the beatific vision. The elevation offered to the creature by God is breathtaking in the extreme. There could be no greater distance between this "natural desire" and participation in the divine being than this.

We have great difficulty, then, in conceiving it. We really only know it is there from the fact that we have been given grace. If we have received it we must have first had a capacity to receive it. However, trying to understand matter, or pure potency in the order of essence, which is of itself unintelligible, is infinitely easier than to understand the openness in the creature to enjoying the life and love of the Creator. To us the most appropriate name for it is "obediential potency". But the "operative" word there is "obediential".

However, in the interpretation of what St. Thomas has to say on this subject, this is not the end of the matter. We have to come to a problem in regard to St. Thomas's other use of the phrase "natural desire" where it seems that he is definitely speaking of "natural" in its ordinary sense, with all its formal and active force. Here we strike a difficulty that has exercised the greatest of minds in the Thomist tradition. For, there is no denying that St. Thomas insists on calling our intellect's potentiality for the beatific vision a natural desire and seems to give it the full status of a positive inclination following a form had. Moreover, he declares quite clearly that the presence of this desire in us can be used, by reason alone, even to demand the positing of our ultimate end as the beatific vision.[9]

It is for this reason that we have said above that the use of this phrase has been an occasion for misunderstanding even by ardent disciples of St. Thomas. How do we reconcile this position of St. Thomas with what we have said above? We believe it can be done. But, it requires us taking an entirely different path, not in pursuing the meaning of natural desire, but the meaning of reason in the context of Theology. The clue to it is to be found in how St. Thomas answers the objection of Richard of St. Victor who would have us believe that we can prove, by reason alone, the existence of the Trinity.

In order to explain how St. Thomas's reliance upon reason to establish the beatific vision as the one final or perfect ultimate end can be reconciled with the explanation we have given, we need to fall back on the distinction he himself makes with regard to the use of reason in sacred theology.

We should be very clear how St. Thomas does argue from reason in this matter pertaining to theology. In fact, in this context he does not say that we can prove apodictically from reason the possibility of our having the beatific vision, or what he calls perfect happiness. He does, however, use a rational argument that we have a natural desire for the beatific vision and that this cannot be futile. So, on the

---

[9]cf. ST, I, 12

face of it, he is relying on reason to establish the possibility of knowledge of the essence of God. [10]

In order to understand what he is doing we need to refer to a principle he has stated about how reason is to be used in relation to matters of faith. This may be seen by his reply to an objection in the *Summa Theologiae*1, 32, 1 ad 2.

"Objection 2. Further, Richard of St. Victor says (De Trin. i, 4): "I believe without doubt that probable and even necessary arguments can be found for any explanation of the truth." So even to prove the Trinity some have brought forward a reason from the infinite good-ness of God, who communicates Himself infinitely in the procession of the divine persons; while some are moved by the consideration that "no good thing can be joyfully possessed without partner-ship."[Note: if we substitute "relationship" for "partnership" we may see this as a quite modern presupposition] then Augustine proceeds (De Trin. x, 4; x, 11,12) to prove the trinity of persons by the proces-sion of the word and of love in our own mind; and we have followed him in this (27, 1 and 3). Therefore the trinity of persons can be known by natural reason.

Reply to Objection 2. Reason may be employed in two ways to establish a point: firstly, for the purpose of furnishing sufficient proof of some principle, as in natural science, where sufficient proof can be brought to show that the movement of the heavens is always of uniform velocity. *Reason is employed in another way, not as fur-nishing a sufficient proof of a principle, but as confirming an already*

---

[10]cf. ST, I, 32, 1

established principle, by showing the congruity of its results, as in astrology the theory of eccentrics and epicycles is considered as established, because thereby the sensible appearances of the heavenly movements can be explained; not, however, as if this proof were sufficient, forasmuch as some other theory might explain them. In the first way, we can prove that God is one; and the like. In the second way, reasons avail to prove the Trinity ; as, when assumed to be true, such reasons confirm it. We must not, however, think that the trinity of persons is adequately proved by such reasons. This becomes evident when we consider each point; for the infinite goodness of God is manifested also in creation, because to produce from nothing is an act of infinite power. For if God communicates Himself by His infinite goodness, it is not necessary that an infinite effect should proceed from God: but that according to its own mode and capacity it should receive the divine goodness. Likewise, when it is said that joyous possession of good requires partnership, this holds in the case of one not having perfect goodness: hence it needs to share some other's good, in order to have the goodness of complete happiness. Nor is the image in our mind an adequate proof in the case of God, forasmuch as the intellect is not in God and ourselves univocally. Hence, Augustine says (Tract. xxvii. in Joan.) that by faith we arrive at knowledge, and not conversely." (italics added)

Now let us look at the article in q.12 of the *Summa Theologiae,* which seems most clearly to prove from reason the possibility of our seeing God's essence.

"I answer that, Since everything is knowable according as it is actual, God, Who is pure act without any admixture of potentiality, is in Himself supremely knowable. But what is supremely knowable in itself, may not be knowable to a particular intellect, on account of the excess of the intelligible object above the intellect; as, for example, the sun, which is supremely visible, cannot be seen by the bat by reason of its excess of light.

Therefore, some who considered this, held that no created intellect can see the essence of God. This opinion, however, is not tenable. For as the ultimate beatitude of man consists in the use of his highest function, which is the operation of his intellect; if we suppose that the created intellect could never see God, it would either never attain to beatitude, or its beatitude would consist in something else beside God; which is opposed to faith. For the ultimate perfection of the rational creature is to be found in that which is the principle of its being; since a thing is perfect so far as it attains to its principle.

Further the same opinion is also against reason. For there resides in every man a natural desire to know the cause of any effect which he sees; and thence arises wonder in men. But if the intellect of the rational creature could not reach so far as to the first cause of things, the natural desire would remain void.

Hence it must be absolutely granted that the blessed see the essence of God."[11] (italics added)

This proof from reason of the possibility of the beatific vision clearly falls within the second way of the employment of reason explained in q.32. How weak this use of reason is from a purely philosophical point of view is evident from the example used by St.

---

[11] ST, I, 12, a1. "Whether any created intellect can see God".

Thomas, where our rational powers were used to "prove" the truth of an integral part of an astronomical theory that is now universally discredited.

It is quite evident, however, that the notion of natural desire relied upon by St. Thomas in the rational argument, which he uses in article 1 above, is a natural desire in the usual sense of an inclination following a form had – a natural inclination in the power of intellect as a quality for its understanding of the forms of things. It does not fit the notion of obediential potency expounded above.

Some wish to interpret it as referring to a desire that is inefficacious and conditional. That might be the case if the possession of the object were regarded as naturally impossible, as if one desired to be able to fly like a bird. But St. Thomas is taking it on the supposition that it is not impossible, known from Faith. He is then applying the natural desire in the intellect to know the causes of things to the first cause that is God. This natural desire, however, only arises in the natural reason on the supposition it is not impossible to know the essence of the First Cause. It is this natural desire that would be rendered void if frustrated.

In the purely natural order of things it is evident that it is impossible to know the essence of God (other than in terms of his effects). It is also not known, nor knowable, that this impossibility might be overcome by help, even divine. From this it follows that no such natural desire would be in the intellect, in respect of the first cause, since one has no natural desire for the naturally impossible.

But, granted the possibility of knowing the essence of God, which we can only know from Faith, St. Thomas is applying the natural inclination of the intellect to know the causes of things to show that reason supports Faith. If the intellect could know the essence of the first cause would it not desire to do so from its inquiring nature? That to us is the force of St. Thomas's appeal to reason to meet the rational objection that we cannot know the essence of God. The argument is not meant to proceed without our knowing from Faith something of the essence of this supreme supernatural end (the beatific vision). Once we know of its possibility and attainability, naturally/rationally our intellect could never be satisfied with anything less.

The argument as presented by St. Thomas may appear to rely solely upon our natural knowledge. But, given the supernatural nature of the subject matter and the theological context, it cannot be treated as if it were apodictic from a purely rational point of view. For, from the point of view of pure reason, direct knowledge of the essence of God is not available to us. Moreover, it pertains to the essence of God to be a trinity of persons. St. Thomas has already shown that this cannot be known by natural reason and *a fortiori* that the three divine persons cannot be objects of a natural desire. As the argument is used, however, it does presuppose that such knowledge of a supernatural end is within our reach.

It is in this context, too, that we have to understand St. Thomas's reference to the divine help that is nonetheless still required by us to achieve the end of our "natural desire". Without knowing of God's positive decree from eternity to raise us to this divine state of happiness (which we can only know from Revelation) it would be presumptuous of us to positively desire it. Nor can we suppose that, before it's possibility is known, there would be such help given.

Healy has said:

"According to the interpretation of de Lubac, in the existing providential order, God has created human beings with a natural desire for a beatitude that as a matter of fact can only be attained through the "second gift" of deifying grace. The desire for beatitude that God has inscribed in nature is a sign that the first gift is made for the second gift. By the same token, the natural desire for the vision of God ensures that the grace bestowed in and through Jesus Christ represents a surpassing but genuine fulfillment of human nature. For de Lubac the paradox and nobility of human existence is seen in human nature's having been created for an ultimate end that is radically beyond human nature."[12]

This is an example of arguing in relation to a matter of the natural order of creation from a supernatural stand point we referred to at the beginning. We can say that "in the existing providential order" God created human beings with a natural desire for beatitude (beatific vision) that can only be attained though grace. But the argument proceeds as if this ordination to grace is the reason for the creation of this natural desire in us. As explained, the desire, properly understood, is natural to us independently of any supernatural ordination, just as the obediential potency to be used by the poet belongs to the ink and lead regardless of whether it is ever so used. By itself, it is not an indication that there is any "supernatural" end. That it should acquire such an end is entirely a matter of the free decision of the higher agency.

---

[12]Healy,"Nature and Grace", 541.

Following St. Thomas's lead in this regard, but without noting the secondary character of the reasoning, all the reasoning of de Lubac and Healy rests on the supposition that God has freely willed (from eternity) to endow created spiritual reality with the grace whereby it becomes ordered to the vision of God. The employment of natural desire in that way of reasoning, however, is a case of reason being "employed in another way, not as furnishing a sufficient proof of a principle, but as confirming an already established principle, by showing the congruity of its results".

The natural desire that is prior to grace is that understood properly as obediential. It is not a sign that the first gift (creation) is made for the second (beatific vision), no more than the nature of heat is made simply for assisting in the process of nourishing the animal (an example St. Thomas gives). That higher function and end comes to heat only from its use by the higher natural living agent. Heat naturally has its own natural form and action and needs to be specially applied by a higher agent to this higher use. Similarly, spiritual nature has its own natural finality and a special ordination (entirely free) by God is required to be had before we can say it is made for the higher divine end of the beatific vision.

De Lubac tries to distinguish a natural condition of human nature without such "natural desire" towards the supernatural end as pertaining to some other "providential order". But so far as human nature is concerned it would be the same in any providential order. The providential order refers to ends, which may be natural but then may also be supernatural. The grace bestowed does indeed represent a surpassing fulfillment of human nature but this does not mean, as the language of fulfillment suggests, that human nature would somehow lack an ultimate natural end without grace. Grace is something that surpasses the natural fulfillment. Lead has its place in the natural constitution of the world without it necessarily being used (in pencils) to write poetry.

When compared to the beatific vision the natural happiness to which we are naturally ordered pales into insignificance. But, we ought to consider it independently of the freely given grace. The very meaning of natural happiness means the fulfillment of all our natural desires. This is also an indication that natural desire as relative to supernatural happiness is no ordinary natural desire, for from its very nature it does not need to be fulfilled for us to be naturally happy.

De Lubac has therefore been unable to dissociate the notion of natural desire in a soul which with the help of God can attain the most perfect ultimate end and that same desire, properly understood as a mere capacity or openness to the action of a superior agent, that does not receive such help because it has not been freely offered.

The argument from the natural desire of the intellect has some force in the context of theology. It is of no apodictic force in a purely philosophical context, as is apparent from St. Thomas's example of the conclusions to be arrived at upon the supposition of the truth of Ptolemy's theory. It is to be noted carefully, however, that "natural desire" as used in the context of the intellect is not the same as used in the context of human nature itself, which is where grace is had.

It is therefore only in the context of Faith that we can use St. Augustine's famous expression: "You have made us for yourself, O

Lord, and our hearts will not rest until they rest in you," as applying to the beatific vision. The desire and hope so expressed supposes and follows upon a free positive divine decree, "the existing providential order" (if from eternity). But having been made it is almost inconceivable to us now that it might not have been made, such is the insight it gives us into the infinite depth of divine love. Accordingly, we tend to take St. Augustine's statement as absolute.

At this point we should note the places where Healy does express de Lubac's position as virtually corresponding to the one we are defending. Thus Healy says:

"Created in the image of God, human beings are by nature capax Dei; this capacity is not yet grace, but defines our nature itself as a non-anticipating readiness for God's gracious and unmerited self-communication in Christ".[13]

What would be a non-anticipating natural desire if not an indeterminate or purely passive one?

Again he says:

"If human nature desires a final end that exceeds nature, then the form of nature's desire is receptivity—a receptive desire for the surprising and surpassing gift of friendship and assistance from another."[14]

Receptivity signifies simply a purely passive attitude, without any active role implied.

Healy further says:

---

[13]Healy, "Nature and Grace", 541-42.
[14]Healy, "Nature and Grace", 561.

"The fact that the nature of spiritual being, as it actually exists, is not conceived as an order destined to close in finally upon itself, but in a sense open to an inevitably supernatural end, does not mean that it already has in itself, or as part of its basis, the smallest supernatural element (MS, 31). The desire itself ... does not constitute as yet even the slightest positive 'ordering' to the supernatural (MS, 85)."[15]

Again he comes close to what we have said about obediential potency:

"The natural desire to see God is interwoven with our innate capacity to attain esse (in this life by a process of metaphysical separatio). But just as created essence has no prior claim to God's bestowal of esse—since it does not exist prior to that bestowal—the natural desire to see God, which is rooted in and expresses our essence as intellectual creatures, does not constitute a "demand" or an "anticipation" of grace. On the contrary, it is a receptive readiness rooted in the fact of having already been given the gift of esse absolutely gratis."[16]

Note, however, how he conflates the two meanings of natural desire that we have been at pains to distinguish, that of the truly obediential/purely passive desire in human substantial nature and that of the suppositional intellectual/active desire in the human intellect (which is in the order of accident).

---

[15]Healy, "Nature and Grace", 550, note 36. Healy is here citing de Lubac's "Mystery of the Supernatural" which he abbreviates to MS.

[16]Healy, "Nature and Grace", 547.

Yet, reverting to the opposite position, allowing for some active contribution on the part of the recipient, Healy expresses himself in this way: "God has freely *inscribed in nature itself*, prior to grace, *a finality* and a desire that goes beyond nature".[17] (italics added)

The use of terms such as "finality", "inscribed" indicate one is thinking in terms of "forms" and "(infra) structures" which can only relate to the supernatural end positively and determinatively (which is what grace brings about).

One suspects that there is present here also a misunderstanding of the notion of potency. Indeed, here one detects a basic metaphysical failing to understand the difference between form and matter; for the desire or inclination that has to be understood lies on the side of potency or matter, receptivity, not act or form, activity. The shade of Suarez continues to hang over the mind of many a modern theologian (particularly strong it seems among the Jesuits).

So it is that de Lubac's notion of the natural desire for the beatific vision oscillates between a purely passive capacity (which is in our view the right interpretation) and one that is not purely passive (which we contend is the fundamental error in his position).

Healy goes on to say:

"The disproportion between human nature's desire and its power to fulfil it is a kind of created *infrastructure* that opens nature from within to receive and participate in the new and unimagined gift of deification. This does not mean, however, that grace arrives at the point where nature breaks down. Rather, it means that grace pre-

---

[17]Healy,"Nature and Grace", 551.

supposes, activates, and fulfils a receptivity (*which involves giving and receiving*) that represents human nature at its highest pitch. The archetype of nature's *active receptivity* is the fiat of Mary which "was decisive, on the human level, for the accomplishment of the divine mystery" (*Redemptoris Mater,* 13)."[18] (italics added)

However, the initial openness to the reception of grace is prior (ontologically) to grace and involves no action or giving on our part. Our giving consent to God's invitation to share in divine life comes from grace, as does the fiat of Mary, if both also involve freedom of will. Indeed, in the same paragraph of the encyclical the pope says: "this response of faith included both perfect cooperation with "the grace of God that *precedes* and assists".[19] (italics added)

Healy also says:

"According to de Lubac, the system of "pure nature" prepared the soil for contemporary secularism insofar as it precluded the idea that the mystery of Jesus Christ reveals the original purpose and meaning of creation itself—reveals, we might say, the nature of nature."[20]

This shows Healy's confusion about the meaning of nature, in which he follows de Lubac. To say that the notion of "pure nature" precludes the supernatural order of grace is pure nonsense. One might as well say that the notion of "pure reason" precludes Faith. Does Faith reveal the reason of reason? Secularism is a philosophy in which reason is so understood as to exclude Faith. That is a dis-

---

[18]Healy, "Nature and Grace", 561-62.
[19]*Redemptoris Mater*, 13.
[20]Healy, "Nature and Grace", 545.

torted notion of reason. So, too, secularism, as naturalism, in which nature is so understood as to exclude "the mystery of Jesus Christ", has a distorted notion of nature.

It is, however, how de Lubac seems to have conceived the concept of nature and the natural, influenced too much by the materialism underlying modern science. He went on then to mistakenly accuse Garrigou-Lagrange and others of fostering secularism by attributing to them this distorted notion of "pure nature"!

By Revelation only we know that God's purpose was not limited to the natural order in creation but also included the elevation of the spiritual order to knowledge and enjoyment of the divine. The act of creation may be one free act of the divine but the order created is twofold, and really distinct, an order confined to merely natural existence and an order super-ordained to a supernatural existence. Even within the natural order, we are able to make these distinctions of orders, e.g. between material and spiritual creation. The fact that the two are by the one act of creation does not mean that the higher precludes the lower, or the lower precludes the higher.

It is not necessary that the mystery of Jesus Christ be "included" in the very notion of nature ("the nature of nature"). The recognition of the values of (human) nature and secularity derived from God himself by creation is not the problem with contemporary secularism but the rejection of the values of faith. De Lubac and his followers seem not to understand the difference between secularity and secularism.

Healy makes comment upon what he calls Feingold's overly doctrinal reading of St. Thomas in comparison with the method of de

Lubac who read him as part of the tradition of Catholic theology. As Healy puts it:

"de Lubac's understanding of theology precludes "any overly preferential attachment to one school, system, or definite age," focusing instead on "the deep and permanent unity of the faith, the mysterious relationship ... of all those who invoke the name of Christ."[21]

It seems that the fault in Feingold and those in the same "scholastic" tradition of reading St. Thomas is that they dwell too exclusively upon extracting the truth of what St. Thomas says rather than interpreting him as situated in the whole stream of theological investigation from the Fathers to the present time. Perhaps unwittingly, there is the subtle suggestion here that we cannot arrive at any definite truth by the study of any author or "school" by itself. Schools and systems are of a "definite age".

What is involved here is the setting up of a false antithesis of methods of study or "reading". Two things are involved in the study of any subject. One is becoming familiar with what those of any standing have said on a matter in question, whether historically or contemporaneously; the other is coming to an understanding of the answer to the question, or the truth of the matter. Both are necessary, but the latter is undoubtedly the primary object of study, and the former is engaged in wholly for the purpose of the second.

Feingold may be said to concentrate on the primary object of study. That is hardly a cause for criticism, especially when the sec-

---

[21]Healy, "Nature and Grace", 538.

ondary object is opposed to it as somehow superior. If anything, Healy's description of de Lubac's approach plays down the idea that any "school" or "system" of thought may contain an inherited treasury of truth. It is only because St. Thomas's system is universally recognised as doing so that so much attention is given to what he says, and not so much to who or where he got it from.

It is very fashionable today to subtly deny the possibility of arriving at any "final truth", taken in the meaning of the final truth on any question, so that the only genuine exercise in scholarship is "research" into the opinions expressed "in the tradition". Alasdair McIntyre is a major influence in this regard:

"Yet to each question the answer produced by Aquinas as a conclusion is no more than and, given Aquinas's method, cannot but be no more than, the best answer reached so far. And hence derives the essential incompleteness. ... except for the finality of Scripture and dogmatic tradition there is and can be no finality."[22]

It seems that today even theologians have begun to absorb the insidious sceptical state of the modern academic mind. We are not saying that de Lubac was necessarily affected in this way, but the excessively traditionalist or exclusively historical approach is a symptom of this relativist influence. In the "new theology" this philosophical traditionalism or historicism is manifested in the opinion that our ability to reach any "final" truth is confined to matters of Faith.

---

[22] Alasdair McIntyre, *Three Rival Versions of Moral Enquiry: Encyclopaedia, Genealogy, and Tradition.* Notre Dame Press, 1990. 123-24.

Feingold's method of reading of him would be defended by St. Thomas himself, one of whose most famous sayings is: "*Studium philosophiae non est ad hoc quod sciatur quid homines senserint, sed qualiter se habeat veritas rerum.*"[23] The study of philosophy is not for this to know what men have thought, but how the truth of things is had.(translation mine)

There remain some further points that can be made but they are basically covered in what has already been said. We should perhaps allude to the fact that de Lubac accepts a twofold happiness but he insists upon calling natural happiness a penultimate happiness. The natural desire for happiness is then reduced to being twofold. It is obvious that the expression "natural desire" cannot mean the same in both cases.

However, the proper conception of the relation between natural happiness and supernatural happiness is not that of something penultimate (next to final) to something ultimate (final), but of two ultimate (final) ends, one subordinated to the other because applying to things of two orders, one lower than the other. The natural happiness belonging to us would still satisfy all our natural desires, for that is what natural happiness means. It is only on the supposition that there is a higher form of (supernatural) happiness made available by divine free will that it is to be conceived as imperfect.

Before finishing, we might just say something about Healy's explanation of how de Lubac sees the bearing of *Humani generis* (1950) upon his position:

---

[23]*In librum Aristotelis de coelo et mundo commentarium,* I, lect. XXII: ed. *Parmensis,* t. XIX, 1865,58.

"Pius XII writes: 'Others destroy the gratuity of the supernatural order, since God, they say, cannot create intellectual beings without ordering and calling them to the beatific vision' (*Humani generis*, 26). De Lubac *accepts this teaching* as true and as essentially consonant with his writings on the supernatural both prior to and posterior to the promulgation of *Humani generis*. At the same time, de Lubac does not think that this teaching in itself is sufficient to secure the gratuity of the supernatural. Why? *Humani generis* refers to a hypothetical order wherein intellectual beings are not ordered and called to perfect beatitude. However, in the world that God has actually created, "[t]he desire for God is written in the human heart, because man is created by God and for God; and God never ceases to draw man to himself." For de Lubac, the teaching of *Humani generis* helps us to see that it would have been possible for God to create intellectual natures other than they would need to be to play their destined role in a providential economy ordered to deification."[24] (italics added)

However, de Lubac, as explained by Healy, misuses the difference between "hypothetical" and "actual", as de Lubac does with the difference between "abstract" and "concrete". The difference makes no impact or change upon the essences or natures under consideration, nor to the essential or natural inclinations or desires that flow necessarily from such essences or natures. Take human nature. It exists in the mind of God from eternity and making it actual simply gives it existence. Whether it remains only in the mind of God or is creat-

---

[24]Healy, "Nature and Grace", 551-52.

ed (given actual existence) or not makes no difference to its nature. Whatever that nature has as part of its essence, uncreated or created, it ever has and ever will have.

In the divine mind human nature has the same natural desire for the beatific vision as it has when positively willed into existence by God, and thus placed in a providential order. De Lubac seems to think that God could have made another intellectual being without this natural desire for the beatific vision. If this desire belongs naturally to the intellectual beings he created it is absurd to say that it might not belong to some other intellectual beings that he could have created but did not.

All the pope means by saying that "God, they say, cannot create intellectual beings without ordering and calling them to the beatific vision" is that it is wrong to say that God could not create (make actual) intellectual beings in their purely natural state with only their natural happiness. In that state they would still have the "natural desire" for supernatural happiness in the sense of an openness to the beatific vision, but they would not be ordered to it.

Healy quotes further from de Lubac's defence of his position:

"Elsewhere, de Lubac notes that *Humani generis* was 'very different from what some had anticipated: it even caused in them some disappointment ... it is not by chance that it avoids any mention of the famous 'pure nature' that a number of highly placed theologians were accusing me of misunderstanding and which they wanted to have canonized (*Entretiensautour de Vatican* II, 13–14; cited in *Theology in History* [San Francisco: Ignatius Press, 1996], 281')".[25]

The Pope may have avoided using the words "pure nature", but there is no mistaking what he is referring to. It is a sign of a weak defence to address the words used and not their evident meanings.

Finally, we note how in his concluding passages Healy slips back to an active notion rather than a purely passive one:

"Nevertheless, its [nature's] role in constituting the relative perfection of nature in its own order (and the entire natural order itself) helps us understand how this very perfection can be a disponability, an *active readiness* for God -one whose innate character is fully revealed precisely when this readiness is "mobilized" in the Son's assumption of human nature from the "Yes" of his immaculate Mother." ... Our "Yes" or "No" to this question pertains not only to theology, but lays bare the philosophical presuppositions about the nature of nature—and the relevance to it of creation as gift."[26] (italics added)

Then, though using the very phrase "obediential potency" he is constrained to give it an active sense:

"For de Lubac, there is a penultimate end, proportionate to our natural capabilities, albeit "imperfect beatitude," and one final end, which is supernatural. *In the present providential economy*, God *places* in created intellectual nature a natural basis for his call to that end, the issuing of which constitutes a second, ontologically /logically distinct "moment." At the heart of created nature there is

---

[25] Healy, "Nature and Grace", 552.note 41.
[26] Healy, "Nature and Grace", 563.

a kind of receptive readiness, which we could call a "specific obediential potency," except that it is *not merely a passive* non-repugnance."[27]

As we see it, his adding of "non-repugnance" is an indication of a state of mind that does not understand the difference between metaphysical potency and logical negativity. Pure potency is not non-being. That one uses such an expression is but further evidence that, like Suarez, one cannot detach the notion of actual being from real (potential) being.

The reader may readily see from the above analysis of Healy's defence that, as noted by Lonergan, de Lubac's position on this question was more mixed up than anything else. This stems we believe from a misunderstanding of nature, underlying which was a more basic misunderstanding of potency, which of course pertains to Philosophy and Metaphysics, if also indispensible to Sacred Theology.

---

[27] Healy, "Nature and Grace", 562. (italics added)

www.ingramcontent.com/pod-product-compliance
Lightning Source LLC
Chambersburg PA
CBHW070024100426
42740CB00013B/2589

*9 7 9 8 8 8 8 7 0 0 9 3 8 *